Cruise Books of the United States Navy in World War II

A BIBLIOGRAPHY

NAVAL HISTORY BIBLIOGRAPHIES, NO. 2

Cruise Books of the United States Navy in World War II

A BIBLIOGRAPHY

Dean L. Mawdsley, M.D.

Naval Historical Center
Department of the Navy
Washington
1993

Illustrations by John Charles Roach

Library of Congress Cataloging-in-Publication Data

Mawdsley, Dean L.
Cruise books of the United States Navy in World War II : a bibliography / Dean L. Mawdsley.
p. cm.
Includes bibliographical references and index.
ISBN 0-945274-13-0
1. World War, 1939–1945—Naval operations, American—Sources.
2. United States. Navy—History—World War, 1939–1945—Sources.
I. Title.
D773.M358 1993
016.94054'5973—dc20 92-41498

∞ The paper used in this publication meets the requirements for permanence established by the American National Standard for Information Sciences "Permanence of Paper for Printed Library Materials" (ANSI Z 39.48–1984).

Contents

The Author

Dr. Dean L. Mawdsley attended Stanford University and the University of California, San Francisco, where he received his MD degree in 1950. His two-year naval service in the Navy V–12 Program at Carroll College, Helena, Montana, in 1944 and 1945, was followed by a total of two years' service as a physician in the U.S. Army from 1952 to 1954 at Ladd Air Force Base, Fairbanks, Alaska. After completing post-graduate training in surgery at the University of California, San Francisco, he entered private practice.

He is the author of *The America of Eric Sloane: A Collector's Bibliography,* published by the Connecticut Historical Commission in 1990. Dr. Mawdsley, now retired, resides in San Mateo County, California, with his wife, Mary Lou.

Foreword

Specialists in modern naval history recognize that the cruise books produced by ships and other naval units are of major value for their research. Informal and nonofficial in nature (they sometimes are compared to college yearbooks), these publications offer insights into the daily activities and attitudes of naval people from the perspective of a unit's crew. Cruise books dating from the World War II years are rare today, but they are of special note because of the intense interest by veterans, writers, and scholars in a conflict that involved the entire American nation and engulfed most of the rest of the world. This interest is heightened by the series of World War II fiftieth anniversaries being celebrated in the United States and abroad at the present time.

Considering the significance of these sources, the reader will understand why Mr. John Vajda, Director of the Navy Department Library, and I were delighted to learn several years ago that Dean L. Mawdsley, a retired California physician, was preparing a catalog of World War II naval cruise books held by American libraries and collectors. The project grew out of the author's personal book-collecting hobby. But it soon became evident that Dean Mawdsley was the national authority on his subject. The scope of his contribution is indicated by the fact that this bibliography identifies nearly 800 individual cruise books held in fourteen libraries, plus a number of private collections, located throughout the United States. The Naval Historical Center is deeply grateful to Dr. Mawdsley for allowing us to publish his major contribution to the bibliography of United States naval history.

A number of other individuals who became associated with this project deserve acknowledgment. As Dr. Mawdsley notes, the late Charles E. Dornbusch, formerly of the New York Public Library, prepared three union lists of naval and military unit histories in the early 1950s that served as a model for the present work. Within the Naval Historical Center, Dr. Mawdsley worked closely with Mr. Vajda, an accomplished bibliographer himself, who provided invaluable advice and assisted Dr. Mawdsley in consulting the rich cruise book collection of the Navy Department Library. Finally, Ms. Sandra J. Doyle, the Naval Historical Center's Senior Editor, must be singled out for praise. With consummate skill, she guided this complex manuscript through the publication process.

A major goal of the Naval Historical Center is to encourage research in U.S. naval history by disseminating information on the basic sources in that field. As the nation and the United States Navy commemorate the fiftieth anniversary of World War II, we are especially pleased to bring forth a new bibliography of the naval cruise books of that conflict.

DEAN C. ALLARD
Director of Naval History

Preface

This bibliography lists close to 800 souvenir books—or cruise books, as they have been called in the U.S. Navy—issued during and immediately after World War II.

The practice of publishing such books dates back to the early days of the twentieth century. Cruise books were issued for some special event, such as the Great White Fleet sailing around the world or some dignitary traveling on an international cruise. A few were issued for U.S. naval vessels that served in World War I, but this practice was not widespread.

It took the greatest naval war in history, namely World War II, to bring forth the first large group of cruise books. During this war millions of Americans were involved with the United States Navy and the drama of sea warfare, especially in the Pacific campaigns. It was natural for these Americans to want a souvenir book recording the part that their own ship or unit played in World War II.

Cruise books are not official U.S. Navy or government publications. Instead, they were produced from money either in the unit's welfare fund or donated by the crew, and they were initiated and produced by the crew. Frequently, it was the chaplain, medical officer, or a welfare officer who took on the task. Fortunate was the crew who had someone on board with journalism training who could put together the ship's story with candid photos, portraits, and maps of the cruises. The books were then distributed free to each crew member or sold for a nominal price. Some of the books are amateurish; others are remarkably professional.

The cover and size of these books varied greatly. Some were mimeographed by the unit or ship's crew and had only a paper cover. Most were printed by commercial firms in the States and some of these have elaborate covers. A few books were printed in England, New Zealand, or Japan soon after the surrender.

Immediately after the war a number of publishing and printing companies produced more professional books. A few of these companies were Army & Navy Pictorial Publishers (formerly Army & Navy Publishing Co.) of Baton Rouge, Schwabacher-Frey Company of San Francisco, and Newsfoto Publishing Company of San Angelo, Texas.

Although no government funds were ever expended directly on the books, the Navy did encourage personnel to spend time producing them. Surely the Navy realized that these books were good public relations and that they promoted unit morale. They were aimed at the

Navy personnel, their relatives back home, and the taxpayers to whom the Navy would have to go for the funds to maintain a postwar Navy.

During the last forty-five years the cruise book tradition has continued, and some ships produce one almost every year. The books have become larger and more elaborate with color photography—altogether a more professional product. However, the books commemorating World War II have a more spontaneous feel to them and may provide historians with a more intimate view of naval life.

Much credit goes to the well-known bibliographer Charles E. Dornbusch and the New York Public Library for putting together a collection of these World War II souvenir books and for publishing the first bibliography in 1950, entitled *Unit Histories of World War II, United States Army, Air Force, Marines, Navy,* under the auspices of the Army's Chief of Military History. With interest in World War II naval history on the increase more than forty years later, it seems to be an appropriate time to reevaluate and update the data.

In doing so, I have diligently tried to find and examine all cruise books of the World War II era, but am the first to admit that there are more in existence than I have located. Even with large collections now in the Navy Department Library at the Washington Navy Yard, Washington, D.C., and the Nimitz Library at the U.S. Naval Academy, Annapolis, World War II cruise books are hard to find. This is because most were printed in small quantities, especially in the case of smaller ships with their smaller crews. And no single collection is complete or even nearly complete.

To establish a book as an authentic World War II souvenir, or cruise, book as opposed to a unit history, I have used several criteria. The book was produced either by the crew or at the behest of the crew. It was published during or soon after World War II for the benefit of the crew. It was not an official U.S. Navy document. It was not the history of a ship or unit written by an author independently of the crew and crew desires.

Although souvenir books of World War II are generally undated, it is logical to assume that, with the fighting over in September 1945, most were published that year or the next. This assumption is supported by the many advertisements in *All Hands* magazine for these books between 1945 and 1947.

Some ships of the late World War II naval shipbuilding program were not commissioned until after Japan's surrender; nevertheless, I have also included the first cruise books for these ships. The cruise books for units involved in the Bikini atomic bomb tests, Operation Crossroads, are also listed even though this operation took place shortly after the war.

Whenever possible I have examined the books to confirm all data from earlier references. So that researchers may have some idea of the contents of a given book, I have also indicated whether or not the book contains photographs, portraits, maps, rosters, and other useful information.

Because many of these books were self-published by crew members, they often lack standard information and sometimes provide facts not typically found in a book. Sometimes, no copy could be found and the little information on them is taken from earlier references. Other books are in private collections that I was sometimes unable to view. I have often corresponded with the owners of the collections and in such instances was able to provide descriptions. My own collection is carefully detailed and listed as a private collection. If there is no description of the contents or appearance of a book, it means I was unable to check it personally or get this information from another source.

This bibliography is divided into four major sections, following the pattern set by Dornbusch. Section 1 lists ship cruise books in alphabetical order. Section 2 covers naval aviation units, with flying units listed serially by number; air ground bases and commands appear alphabetically. Books issued by naval construction (Seabee) units appear in section 3, presented serially by number, except for the last section, which is in alphabetical order. Books issued by other naval commands make up section 4, classified according to amphibious forces, Coast Guard units, medical facilities, naval officer training units, naval supply units, and other commands. Each subcategory is in alphabetical order.

Coast Guard ships and units serving under the Navy in wartime are included. Marine Corps units, whether ground or air, are not included.

I would greatly appreciate readers' forwarding new information to me on the books listed in this bibliography, or on books that fit the criteria but are omitted altogether. Write to me in care of the Naval Historical Center, Washington, D.C. 20374–0571. A supplement to this bibliography may appear some time in the future.

Acknowledgments

As I began my effort about four years ago to update and expand the information on naval cruise books during World War II, I sought out Charles E. Dornbusch in the Catskill Mountains of New York. Mr. Dornbusch, author of the 1950 original bibliography on this subject, was retired as librarian of the New York Public Library and maintaining a small book shop and publishing business. He was interested in my planned research and encouraged me to proceed. The numerous references to Dornbusch's work in this bibliography attest to the excellent job he did more than forty years ago. It is my regret that he did not live to see this publication.

A number of book dealers specializing in naval and aeronautic books have directed me to other collectors and called my attention to books that I had not as yet included in my developing bibliography. Among those most helpful were William Byrd, Los Angeles; Dan F. Webb, Oakland; George Kastner, Los Osos, California; C. D. Perrotti, Londonderry, New Hampshire; and Paul Gaudette, Tucson, Arizona.

I refrain from mentioning the many private collectors who have given me helpful information. I do so to protect their privacy, and not from any lack of appreciation for their contributions.

The government libraries with cruise book collections have been my most valuable source of information. John P. Cummings, associate librarian of the Nimitz Library at the U.S. Naval Academy; Dan Roth, Curator of the Navy Supply Corps Museum; Dr. Vincent Transano, Director of the Civil Engineer Corps–Seabee Museum; Ken Snyder of the National Museum of Naval Aviation; William P. Galvani, Director of the Submarine Force Library and Museum; Evelyn M. Cherpak, Archivist of the Naval War College; Jan Herman, Historian of the Naval Medical Command Archives; and Edward Von der Porten, Director of the Treasure Island Museum.

The staffs of the New York Public Library, Mystic Seaport Library, and Admiral Nimitz State Historical Park were also most helpful.

A special note of appreciation goes to James T. Controvich. He graciously shared with me an unpublished manuscript that listed most of the World War II cruise books. This manuscript has been valuable for adding new material and also for cross-checking my own manuscript.

I wish especially to acknowledge the help and encouragement of Dr. Dean C. Allard, Director of Naval History, and John Vajda, Director of the Navy Department Library, both at the Navy Yard, Naval Historical Center, Washington, D.C. They and their staffs spared no effort to bring this project to fruition. Thanks go to John Charles Roach who donated his time and talents to illustrate this work and to SSR, Incorporated, especially its editors, Karen L. Plante and Steve Yoder, who copy edited the manuscript and prepared it for printing. Their cooperation and encouragement are greatly appreciated. I am also indebted to Dr. Allard for his Foreword to this book.

Explanatory Notes

Brackets. Information in brackets has been obtained from a source other than the book itself. A date with a question mark in brackets indicates the date is estimated.

Titles. In some cases, the title on the title page differs from the cover title; sometimes the spine of the book has still another title. When more than one title appears, the first one listed is taken from the title page; this is the title librarians use in cataloging. Titles taken from other locations in the book are so designated.

Facts of publication. Because some of the facts of publication may be missing, n.p. is used to indicate that no place of publication is given, and n.d. indicates no date appears or has been estimated. A company name may be the publisher of the book, it may be the printer of the book, or it may be a company that handles both functions; the last two are unusual facts to give in a book.

Description. Cover sizes are stated in centimeters (cm), with the vertical measure appearing before the horizontal. If only one number is listed, it is the vertical dimension.

References. If a book has been mentioned in an earlier publication, that reference is noted.

Copy location. Facilities known to have a copy of the book are listed by the following abbreviations:

BMA	Bureau of Medicine and Surgery Archives, Washington, D.C. 20372–5120
MSL	Mystic Seaport Library, Mystic Seaport Museum, Mystic, Connecticut 06355–1961
NDL	Navy Department Library, Building 44, Washington Navy Yard, Washington, D.C. 20374–0571
NSP	Admiral Nimitz State Historical Park, 340 E. Main Street, Fredericksburg, Texas 78624–4612
NWC	Naval War College Library, Newport, Rhode Island 02841–5010
NYPL	New York Public Library, Fifth Avenue and 42nd Street, New York, New York 10018–2788
PNAM	National Museum of Naval Aviation, Naval Air Station, Pensacola, Florida 32508–6800
SCM	Navy Supply Corps Museum, Athens, Georgia 30606–5000

SFL	Submarine Force Library and Museum, Crystal Lake Road, Groton, Connecticut 06349–5000
SMPH	Civil Engineer Corps–Seabee Museum, Naval Construction Battalion Center, Port Hueneme, California 93043–5000
TIL	Treasure Island Museum, Building 1, Treasure Island, San Francisco, California 94130–5018
USCGA	U.S. Coast Guard Academy Library, New London, Connecticut 06320–4197
USCGPA	U.S. Coast Guard, Public Affairs Division, Department of Transportation, Washington, D.C. 20593–0001
USNA	Nimitz Library, U.S. Naval Academy, Annapolis, Maryland 21402–5029

References

All Hands: The Bureau of Naval Personnel Information Bulletin. Washington: Bureau of Naval Personnel, Department of the Navy, published monthly.

Antheil Booksellers Catalogue. North Bellmore, N.Y.

Books Published by Army & Navy Publishing Company. Baton Rouge: Army & Navy Publishing Co.

Controvich, James T. *The Central Pacific Campaign, 1943–1944: A Bibliography.* Westport, Conn.: Meckler, 1990.

Controvich, James T. "United States Navy, Marine Corps & Coast Guard Unit & Organizational Histories, World War II Era." Unpublished manuscript, 1992.

Dabney Catalogues of Old, Rare, Used, and Out-of-Print Books on Military History. Washington: Q. M. Dabney & Co.

Dornbusch, Charles E. *Unit Histories of World War II: United States Army, Air Force, Marines, Navy.* Washington: Office of the Chief of Military History, Department of the Army, 1950.

Dornbusch, Charles E. *Supplement 1951 to Unit Histories of World War II: United States Army, Air Force, Marine Corps, Navy 1950.* Washington: Office of the Chief of Military History, Department of the Army, September 1951.

Paul Gaudette Books Catalogues. Tucson: Paul Gaudette Books.

Smith, Myron J. *World War II at Sea: A Bibliography of Sources in English.* 3 vols. Metuchen, N.J.: Scarecrow Press, 1976.

Zeigler, Janet. *World War II: Books in English, 1945–65.* Stanford, Calif.: Hoover Institution Press, 1971.

1

Ship Books

Aaron Ward (DM 34)

1 *USS Aaron Ward* (cover). Lt. L. Lavrakas, ed. N.p., [1946?]. 40 pp., heavy white paper cover with blue printing and decoration, 28.1 x 22.8 cm, photos, ports., map, roster. NDL.

Abbot (DD 629)

2 *History of the U.S.S. Abbot DD 629*. Anon. Foreword by Comdr. F. W. Ingling. N.p., [1945?]. 48 pp., orange hardcover, 21.5 x 14.5 cm. USNA.

Adair (APA 91)

3 *USS Adair APA 91: Photographs of an 18-Month Cruise During World War II Presented to Her Crew*. Anon. N.p., [1945?]. Unpaged, paper cover, 21 x 26.7 cm. NDL, NWC.

Admiral E. W. Eberle (AP 123)

4 *USS Admiral E. W. Eberle AP–123*. Anon. Portland, Oreg.: T. G. Merkley Co., [1945?]. 48 leaves, blue hardcover with gold printing and silhouette of *Eberle,* loose-leaf binding, 22.8 x 28.8 cm, photos, ports., map, roster. Dornbusch 1950: 838, Smith: 7043. USCGPA.

Admiral R. E. Coontz (AP 122)

5 *Diary, U.S.S. Admiral Coontz*. Anon. Portland, Oreg.: T. G. Merkley Co., 1946. 56 leaves, 23 x 29 cm, photos, ports., maps. Dornbusch 1950: 837. NYPL.

Admiral W. L. Capps (AP 121)

6 *U.S.S. Admiral W. L. Capps AP–121: A Pictorial History of the Coast Guard Manned Navy Transport U.S.S. W. L. Capps AP–121*. Anon. N.p., [1946?]. 55 leaves, 21 x 26 cm, photos. Dornbusch 1951 supp: 1462. NDL, NYPL (photocopy).

Admiral W. S. Benson (AP 120)

7 Listed in *Antheil Booksellers Catalogue* in 1967, 1968, 1969.

Alabama (BB 60)

8 *War Diary, USS Alabama, 1942–1944*. Anon. N.p., [1946?]. 68 leaves, light blue hardcover with drawing of *Alabama* pasted on and title printed in gold, 27.3 x 21.7 cm, photos, ports., map, roster. Dornbusch 1950: 839, Smith: 7051. NDL, USNA.

Alaska (CB 1)

9 *U.S.S. Alaska (CB 1), "Memories" 17 June 1944–18 December 1945.* Cover: U.S.S. Alaska CB1. Anon. N.p., [1945?]. 64 leaves, blue hardcover with gold printing, 20.2 x 27.2 cm, photos, ports., map. Dornbusch 1950: 840, Smith: 7052. NDL, USNA.

Alcyone (AKA 7)

10 *The Saga of an AKA.* Cover: U.S.S. Alcyone AKA 7. Anon. Philadelphia: Campus Publishing Co., 1945. 32 leaves, embossed blue hardcover with gold printing and silhouette of AKA 7, 28.7 x 22.3 cm, photos, ports., map, roster. Dornbusch 1950: 841. NDL, NYPL.

Alfred A. Cunningham (DD 752)

11 *Alfred A. Cunningham, Destroyer DD–752.* Anon. N.p., [1945?]. Unpaged, 28 x 22 cm, USNA (rebound).

Alkes (AKA 110)

12 *Alkes Album, November 1945.* Cover: Alkes Album. Anon. Long Beach, Calif.: Robinson Printing & Stationery Co., 1945. 64 pp., embossed blue hardcover with gold printing and drawing of ship, 26.0 x 20.7 cm, photos, ports. Private collection.

Ammen (DD 527)

13 *The United States Ship Ammen, March 12, 1943–April 15, 1946.* Cover: The Mighty A. Anon. Charleston: Walker, Evans & Cogswell Co., [1946?]. 45 pp., blue hardcover with embossed title, 29 cm, photos, ports. Dornbusch 1950: 842, Smith: 7059. NDL, USNA.

Anne Arundel (AP 76)

14 *U.S.S. Anne Arundel (AP–76).* Cover: P 76. Lt. Henry C. Gulbandson, USNR. Tacoma, Wash.: Johnson-Cox Co., [1945?]. 103 pp., blue hardcover with gold printing, 23.7 x 30.5 cm, photos, ports., map, roster. Dornbusch 1950: 843, Smith: 7063. NDL, USNA.

Anthony (DD 515)

15 *The Mad Anthony: The Story of a Ship and Her Men.* Cover: The Mad Anthony. Anon. Charleston, S.C.: Southern Printing & Publishing Co., [1946?]. 24 pp., blue paper cover with red and white printing and decoration, 26.5 x 20.7 cm, photos, roster. Dornbusch 1950: 844, Smith: 7064. NDL, NYPL.

ARD Ten

16 *ARD Ten*. Anon. N.p., 1945. This citation was taken from NDL card file although copy could not be located in NDL. No other known reference. Title may refer to a floating drydock.

Arkansas (BB 33)

17 *USS Arkansas, Pictorial Review, 1944*. Anon. Foreword by the chaplain. N.p., 1944. 64 pp., 31 x 22 cm. Smith: 7068. USNA (rebound).

18 *U.S.S. Arkansas Pacific War Diary*. Lt. H. A. Wilson, ed. N.p., [1946?]. 56 leaves, blue cover with gold and blue printing, 27.2 x 21.4 cm, photos, ports., map. Dornbusch 1950: 845, Smith: 7067. NDL, USNA (rebound).

Ashtabula (AO 51)

19 *USS Ashtabula (AO 51): Her History*. Ens. John Edward Weeks. N.p., 1946. Unpaged, photos, ports., officer roster, itinerary, list of ships refueled. NSP (photocopy).

Astoria (CA 34)

20 *USS Astoria CA–34, 1934–1942*. Ken Cruse, ed. N.p., [1942?]. 48 leaves, blue-gray softcover with black printing and photograph of CA 34, 27.5 x 21 cm, photos, map, roster. NDL.

Astoria (CL 90)

21 *The First Cruise of the U.S.S. Astoria*. Cover: Mighty Ninety. Anon. Long Beach: Green's, [1946?]. 40 leaves, blue hardcover with gold printing, 16 x 24 cm, photos, ports. Dornbusch 1950: 846, Smith: 7073. NDL, NYPL.

Atlanta (CL 104)

22 *U.S.S. Atlanta: A Travelogue . . . September 22, 1947 to May 12, 1948*. Cover: U.S.S. Atlanta, China Cruise. Anon. Los Angeles: Metropolitan Engravers, [1948?]. 27.3 x 20.3 cm, photos, ports., map, roster. NYPL. This is the first cruise book in the early post-WW II period for one of the later units of the *Cleveland* class.

Attu (CVE 102)

23 *Cruise of the "Little A"*. Lt.(jg) E. G. Burrows, ed. Sacramento: Bee Engraving and News Publishing Co., [1945?]. 32 leaves, blue hardcover with silver printing and decoration, 28 x 22 cm, photos, ports., map. USNA.

Ault (DD 698)

24 *U.S.S. Ault DD 698: A War History of U.S.S. Ault* (cover). Anon. N.p., [1945?]. 13 pp., printed on one side of sheet only, buff paper cover with black printing and photo of DD 698, 20.4 x 15.6 cm, photos. Dornbusch 1950: 847, Smith: 7074. NDL.

Bairoko (CVE 115)

25 *Album, USS Bairoko CVE 115*. Anon. Baton Rouge: Army & Navy Pictorial Publishers, 1946. 56 leaves, 30.7 x 23.1 cm, blue hardcover with gold printing, photos, ports., map. Dornbusch 1950: 848, Smith: 7080. NDL.

Baltimore (CA 68)

26 *The History of the USS Baltimore CA–68*. Cover: USS Baltimore CA–68. Anon. San Angelo, Tex.: Newsfoto Publishing Co., [1945?]. 117 leaves, blue hardcover with gold-embossed title and silhouette of CA 68, 20.5 x 27 cm, photos, ports., map. Dornbusch 1950: 849, Smith: 7083. NDL, USNA.

Barnes (CVE 20)

27 *USS Barnes, Escort Carrier CVE–20, 1942–1945*. Cover: USS Barnes. Anon. Layout by Lt. Fred Stewart. San Francisco: Knight-Counihan Co., [1946?]. 40 leaves, dark blue hardcover with light blue printing and photo of ship pasted on, 30.9 x 23.5 cm, photos, ports. Dornbusch 1950: 850, Smith: 7087. NDL, USNA.

Barnett (APA 5)

28 *Department of the Navy, USS Barnett, World War II, 1940–1945: A Pictorial History of the USS Barnett (APA–5)*. Donald W. Boyd, Jr., and E. Parker Osborne, eds. N.p., [1946?]. 28 leaves, blue hardcover with embossed Department of Navy seal, 21.5 x 28.5 cm. Private collection.

Barton (DD 722)

29 *U.S.S. Barton DD 722* (cover). Anon. N.p., [1946?]. 52 leaves, 21 x 33 cm, photos. Dornbusch 1950: 851, Smith: 7090. No known copy location.

Bataan (CVL 29)

30 *The U.S.S. Bataan, 1 August 1943–17 October 1945.* Cover: The Bataan. Anon. Charlotte, N.C.: Observer Printing House, [1946?]. 219 pp., embossed cream and blue hardcover with ship, 31 x 24 cm, photos, ports., roster. Dornbusch 1950: 852, Smith: 7092. NDL, NYPL, USNA (rebound).

Beckham (APA 133)

31 Title unknown. Anon. San Francisco: 1945. 28 leaves, 21 x 31 cm, photos, ports. Dornbusch 1950: 853, Smith: 7101. No known copy location.

Belleau Wood (CVL 24)

32 *"Flight Quarters": The War Story of the U.S.S. Belleau Wood.* Lt. John W. Alexander, ed. Los Angeles: Cole-Holmquist Press, 1946. 190 pp., blue hardcover with gold printing of title and ship, 28 x 21.5 cm, photos, ports., map, roster. Dornbusch 1950: 854, Smith: 7105, Zeigler: 2553. NDL, NWC, USNA.

Benevolence (AH 13)

33 *Ben-Vues—1945: Mementos of Our Ship, the USS Benevolence.* Cover: Ben-Vues, 1945. CPhM J. E. Shaw, et al. N.p., n.d. Unpaged, tan paper cover with photo of ship, 18 x 26 cm, photos, roster. NDL.

Bennington (CV 20)

34 *U.S.S. Bennington CV–20* (cover). Historical and Pictorial Review, U.S.S. Bennington, World War II (top of page 3). Anon. N.p., [1946?]. 66 pp., gray softcover with title and photo of *Bennington,* 30.5 x 23 cm, photos, map, crew roster and casualty list. Dornbusch 1950: 856, Smith: 7108. NDL, NYPL, PNAM, USNA (rebound).

Bennion (DD 662)

35 *The Story of the Bennion.* Anon. N.p., November 1947. 112 pp., light blue hardcover with gold printing and black silhouette of *Bennion*, 28.5 x 22 cm, photos, ports., map, crew roster and casualty list. Dornbusch 1950: 855, Smith: 7109, Zeigler: 2692. NDL, USNA.

Benson (DD 421)

36 *U.S.S. Benson DD–421, 1940–1946* (cover). Anon. San Angelo, Tex.: Newsfoto Publishing Co., [1946?]. 36 leaves, blue hardcover with gold-embossed printing and silhouette of DD 421, 20.5 x 27 cm, photos, ports., map, casualty list. Dornbusch 1951 supp.: 1465, Smith: 7111. NDL, NYPL, USNA.

Biloxi (CL 80)

37 *U.S.S. Biloxi.* Anon. San Francisco: Schwabacher-Frey Co., [1945?]. 44 leaves, dark blue hardcover with gold printing and silhouette of *Biloxi*, 23.5 x 30.8 cm, photos, ports. Dornbusch 1950: 857, Smith: 7117. NDL, USNA.

Birmingham (CL 62)

38 *CL–62: The Saga of the U.S.S. Birmingham, A Compilation of Her Officers & Men.* Cover: USS Birmingham. Anon. San Angelo, Tex.: Newsfoto Publishing Co., [1946?]. 96 leaves, blue hardcover with gold printing and silhouette of CL 62, 20.5 x 27 cm, photos, ports., maps, roster of awards. Dornbusch 1951 supp.: 1465, Smith: 7119. NDL, NYPL.

Black Hawk (AD 9)

39 *U.S.S. Black Hawk, Built 1913, Commissioned May 1918: "Tender Stuff," An Epitaph.* Cover: USS Black Hawk. Anon. N.p., [1946?]. 123 pp., blue hardcover with gold printing and embossed Indian head, 31 x 23.6 cm, photos, ports., map, roster. Private collection.

Block Island (CVE 21) and (CVE 106)

40 *U.S.S. Block Island CVE 21 and CVE 106, United States Navy: The Story of Two Escort Carriers Who Carried the War to the Enemy During Three Years of Conflict.* Anon. New York: Anchor Printing, [1946?]. 33 leaves, blue hardcover, 35 cm, photos, ports., map. Dornbusch 1950: 858, Smith: 7123. NDL, NYPL (film), private collection.

Blue (DD 744)

41 *War Diary of the U.S.S. Blue Destroyer 744*. Anon. Seattle: Sterling Engraving Co., [1946?]. 17 leaves, red hardcover with blue printing and silhouette of *Blue*, 27.1 x 20.7 cm, photos, ports., map, roster. Dornbusch 1950: 859, Smith: 7125. NDL.

Bogue (CVE 9)

42 *U.S.S. Bogue* (cover). Anon. N.p., [1945?]. 48 pp., heavy multi-color paper cover with photograph of *Bogue* and ribbon decoration, 20.7 x 13.5 cm, photos, ports., map, roster of department heads. Dornbusch 1950: 860, Smith: 7130. NDL.

Boston (CA 69)

43 *U.S.S. Boston CA 69* (cover). Henry G. Leader. [San Angelo, Tex.: Newsfoto Publishing Co.] [1945?]. 36 leaves, blue hardcover with gold-embossed printing and silhouette of cruiser, 20.5 x 27.5 cm, photos, ports., map. Dornbusch 1951 supp.: 1466, Smith: 7132. NDL, NYPL, USNA.

Bountiful (AH 9)

44 *The U.S.S. Bountiful (AH–9) in the Pacific, World War II, April 1944 to September 1945*. Compiled by Comdr. Jack C. Morris. Berkeley: Lederer Street & Zeus, [1945?]. 50 pp., 28.4 x 20 cm, photos, ports., medical staff roster. NDL, NYPL.

Bullard (DD 660)

45 *"The Bullard,": The Story of the USS Bullard Destroyer 660 and the Men Who Served on Her*. TM2c Herbert H. Graefe and Lt.(jg) Richard C. Thommen, eds. N.p., [1946?]. 83 pp., dark green hardcover with gold-embossed letters, 21.5 x 28 cm. Private collection.

Bullhead (SS 332)

46 *Overdue and Presumed Lost: The Story of the U.S.S. Bullhead.* Martin Sheridan. Francistown, N.H.: Marshall Jones Co., 1947. 143 pp., Controvich 1992: 27, Dornbusch 1950: 862. No known copy location. This book does not strictly qualify as a cruise book, but is included because it has appeared in earlier bibliographies.

Bunker Hill (CV 17)

47 *A History of the U.S.S. Bunker Hill CV–17, Dec. 1942–Oct. 1945*. Private collection list. No known copy location.

48 *The U.S.S. Bunker Hill, November 1943–November 1944: The Record of a Carrier's Combat Action Against the Axis Nations in the Pacific*. Cover: U.S.S. Bunker Hill, Department of the Navy, November 1943–November 1944. Lt. Wallace C. Mitchell, USNR, and Lt. Eugene F. Brissie, USNR, eds. Chicago: Rogers Printing Co., 1945. 272 pp., maroon hardcover with gold-embossed seal, 31.2 x 23.7 cm, photos, ports., map. Dornbusch 1950: 863, Smith: 7161. NDL, NWC, PNAM, USNA.

Burleson (APA 67)

49 *The Cruise, Published by and for the Crew of the U.S.S. Burleson*. Anon. N.p., [1945?]. 32 leaves, 27 cm, photos, ports. Dornbusch 1950: 864, Smith: 7162. NDL.

Cabot (CVL 28)

50 *U.S.S. Cabot, Unit History*. Anon. N.p., [1946?]. Part I: chronology, 14 pp; Part II: narrative, 62 pp.; Part III: photographs. Unbound softcover, 20.3 x 26.7 cm. NWC. Author has not seen this book, and it may not be a typical cruise book.

California (BB 44)

51 *U.S.S. California: An Account of the Wartime Cruising of the USS California from Pearl Harbor to Tokyo Bay, 7 December 1941–3 October 1945*. Cover: U.S.S. California. Gunnery Sgt. Richard W. Cunningham, USMC, and Lt. William A. Hewitt, USNR. N.p., [1945?]. 124 leaves, blue and white cloth hardcover with gold printing, 22.3 x 28.6 cm, photos, ports., map. Dornbusch 1950: 865, Smith: 7167. NDL (photocopy), NYPL, USNA (rebound).

52 *U.S.S. California: Homeward Bound from Tokyo*. Cover: U.S.S. California. Lt. William A. Hewitt, USNR. N.p.: Stern, [1946?]. 27 leaves, heavy maroon paper cover with blue printing and spiral binding, 22.5 x 29.8 cm, photos, ports. Private collection.

Cape Gloucester (CVE 109)

53 *U.S.S. Cape Gloucester Album: A Pictorial Log*. Anon. Chicago: Rogers Printing Co., [1945?]. 107 pp., 28 cm, photos, ports. Dornbusch 1950: 866, Smith: 7168. No known copy location.

Cascade (AD 16)

54 *U.S.S. Cascade, 1943–1944* (cover). Chaplain W. A. Nicholas, ed. San Francisco: Recorder-Sunset Press, [1945?]. 64 pp., heavy blue paper cover with gold printing and silhouette of *Cascade*, 21.5 x 28.5 cm, photos, ports. Private collection.

Chandeleur (AV 10)

55 *The War Diary of the U.S.S. Chandeleur (AV–10).* Cover: For Auld Lang Syne: U.S.S. Chandeleur, 1942–1945. Anon. San Francisco: Schwabacher-Frey Co., 1946. 71 leaves, blue hardcover with gold printing and *Chandeleur* silhouette, 31.1 x 23.5 cm, photos, ports., map, roster. Dornbusch 1950: 867, Smith: 7183. NDL, USNA.

Charles S. Sperry (DD 697)

56 *Destroyer 697.* John Louis Casey, Jr. Illustrated by Loring Corkum, William Forquer, and Oscar Lefebre. N.p., [1945?]. 28 leaves, 27 cm, photos. Dornbusch 1950: 868, Smith: 7180. NYPL (reproduced from typewritten copy).

Chenango (CVE 28)

57 *The Chenanigan Victory Edition, 1942–1945.* Cover: U.S.S. Chenango C.V.E. 28. Almon B. Ives and Ben A. Meginniss, eds. Los Angeles: Kater Engraving Co., [1945?]. 64 pp., blue softcover with gold printing and cartoon, 27.3 x 21 cm, photos, ports., roster. Dornbusch 1950: 869, Smith: 7186, Zeigler: 2560. NDL (photocopy), USNA (rebound).

Chilton (APA 38)

58 *U.S.S. Chilton Pictorial Log* (cover). Anon. N.p., [1945?]. 37 pp., photos, ports., map. Advertised in *All Hands*, July 1947, NYPL.

Clamp (ARS 33)

59 *History of the U.S.S. Clamp (ARS 33)* (cover). Anon. N.p., [1947?]. 8 pp., paper cover, 26 x 19.3 cm. Advertised in *All Hands*, July 1947. USNA (mimeographed copy of typewritten manuscript received August 1947).

Cleveland (CL 55)

60 *United States Ship Cleveland.* Cover: USS Cleveland. Ens. D. D. Robertson, ed. Andover, Mass.: Andover Press, 1946. 80 pp., blue hardcover with embossed title and U.S. Navy seal, 31 x 23.5 cm, photos, ports., map, roster. Dornbusch 1950: 870, Smith: 7189. NDL, NYPL, USNA.

Cockrill (DE 398)

61 *The Seafarer: Published at Sea by the Men of the Cockrill* (cover). John A. Hafling, ed. N.p., [1946?]. 68 pp., white softcover with blue and black printing, 25.3 x 19.0 cm, photos, ports. Dornbusch 1951 supp.: 1467. USNA.

Colorado (BB 45)

62 *The Colorado Cruise Book*. Cover: U.S.S. Colorado Cruise Book, 1942–1946. Lt. Robert C. Lusk, ed. Seattle: Craftsman, [1946?]. 47 leaves, blue hardcover with gold printing and photograph of *Colorado* on front, 27 x 21.2 cm, photos, ports., map, roster. Dornbusch 1950: 871, Smith: 7194. NDL, NSP, USNA.

Columbia (CL 56)

63 *Battle Record and History of the U.S.S. Columbia, 1942–1945*. Cover: U.S.S. Columbia, 1942–1945. Comdr. F. O. Iffrig et al., eds. Baltimore: Horn Shafer Co., [1945?]. 88 pp., blue hardcover with gold printing, photograph of *Columbia* and battle ribbons, 27.4 x 20.3 cm, photos, ports., maps. Dornbusch 1950: 872, Smith: 7195. NDL, NYPL, USNA.

Comet (AP 166)

64 *Following the Comet's Tale, 1944–1945* (cover). Lt.(jg) R. C. Ferguson, USNR, ed. San Francisco: Schwabacher-Frey Co., 1946. 95 pp., embossed blue cover with gold printing and decoration, 22 x 15.5 cm, photos, ports., map. Dornbusch 1950: 873, Smith: 7196. NDL, NPL, NYPL, USNA.

Commencement Bay (CVE 105)

65 *The Bay Wake: U.S.S. Commencement Bay (CVE 105)*. Cover: Bay Wake. RdM2c John R. Pyburn, ed. Tacoma, Wash.: Johnson-Cox Co., 1946. 76 pp., blue hard plastic-cover with silver printing, 28.9 x 20.9 cm, photos, ports. USNA.

Consolation (AH 15)

66 This citation was taken from NDL card file although copy could not be located in NDL. No other known reference.

Cowpens (CVL 25)

67 *The Story of the U.S.S. Cowpens (CVL–25).* Anon. Baton Rouge: Army & Navy Pictorial Publishers, 1946. 49 pp., 27 cm, photos, ports. Dornbusch 1951 supp.: 1468, Smith: 7209. Private collection (photocopy), PNAM (photocopy).

Custer (APA 40)

68 *U.S.S. Custer* (cover). Anon. N.p., [1946?]. 16 leaves, blue softcover with gold printing, 21 x 14 cm, photos, ports., roster. Dornbusch 1950: 874, Smith: 7217. NDL.

Daly (DD 519)

69 *U.S.S. Daly (DD 519).* Anon. Charleston: Walker, Evans & Cogswell, [1945?]. 94 pp., brown hardcover with embossed title and decoration, 26.3 x 18.3 cm, photos, roster. Dornbusch 1950: 875, Smith: 7219. NDL, NYPL.

Dashiell (DD 659)

70 *The United States Ship Dashiell . . . Her Story.* Cover: U.S.S. Dashiell: Her Story. Anon. Charleston: Walker, Evans & Cogswell, [1945?]. 35 leaves, blue hardcover with black printing and ship silhouette, 28.9 x 22.0 cm, photos, ports., roster. Dornbusch 1950: 876, Smith: 7220. NDL.

Dauphin (APA 97)

71 *Cruise of the U.S.S. Dauphin (Attack Transport No. 97), 23 September 1944 to 20 November 1945.* Cover: U.S.S. Dauphin. Anon. San Francisco: Mercury Press, [1945?]. 120 pp., blue hardcover with gold printing and decoration, 29.5 x 20.5 cm, photos, ports., map, roster. Dornbusch 1950: 877, Smith: 7222. NSP, NYPL, USNA.

Dayton (CL 105)

72 *War Cruise of the U.S.S. Dayton CL–105.* Cover: The Dauntless "D" CL-105. Anon. N.p., [1946?]. 32 leaves, 15 x 23 cm, photos, ports. Dornbusch 1950: 878, Smith: 7229. NDL.

Denver (CL 58)

73 *Life Aboard the U.S.S. Denver: A Biography of the CL 58, 1942–1945.* Cover: Life Aboard the U.S.S. Denver, 1942–1945. Anon. Baltimore: Thomsen-Ellis-Hutton Co., [1946?]. 40 pp., blue hardcover with gold printing and silhouette of CL 58, 27.8 x 20.3 cm, photos, ports., map. Dornbusch 1950: 879, Smith: 7231, NDL, NYPL.

Duluth (CL 87)

74 *U.S.S. Duluth: A Short History.* Cover: U.S.S. Duluth. Anon. N.p., [1945?]. 15 leaves, gray hardcover with black and red printing, 15.3 x 23.4 cm, photos, ports. Private collection.

Dutchess (APA 98)

75 *History of the U.S.S. Dutchess APA–98, August 1944–March 1945.* Lt. Comdr. Raymond Stevenson, USNR. Norfolk: Phaup Printing Co., [1946?]. 89 pp., rebound in blue hardcover, 23 x 16 cm, photos, ports., roster. NDL, USNA. Author has not seen original cover.

Dyson (DD 572)

76 *U.S.S. Dyson Destroyer 572.* Anon. Philadelphia: Campus Publishing Co., [1946?]. 24 leaves, blue hardcover with gold-embossed title and decoration, 27.3 x 20 cm, photos, ports., map, roster. USNA.

Edgecomb (APA 164)

77 *United States Ship Edgecomb.* Cover: Amphibious Attack Transport U.S.S. Edgecomb APA 164, 1945. Cpl. Robert J. W. Lund, USAAF, ed. N.p., [1946?]. 32 leaves, printed on one side of sheet only, blue softcover with silver printing, 27 x 20.6 cm, photos, ports., map, roster. Dornbusch 1950: 881, Smith: 7247, NDL.

Eldorado (AGC 11)

78 *USS Eldorado 1945, AGC 11 Flagship* (cover). Anon. Printed on board 1945. 48 pp., green and blue softcover with bow view of *Eldorado,* 26.5 x 20.4 cm, ports., photos, map. NDL, private collection.

Elizabeth C. Stanton (AP 69)

79 *U.S.S. Elizabeth C. Stanton* (cover). Lt. Kenneth A. Berg, ed. N.p., [1945?]. 112 pp., green hardcover with gold printing, 28.5 x 20.9 cm, photos, ports., roster. Dornbusch 1950: 882, Smith: 7251, NDL.

Enterprise (CV 6)

80 *Saga of the U.S.S. Enterprise*. Anon. New York: N.p., 1945. 8 leaves, 20 cm. Dornbusch 1950: 883, Smith: 7255. No known copy location.

81 *History of the U.S.S. Enterprise (CV–6)* (cover). Anon. N.p., [1946?]. 23 pp., white paper cover with black printing, 19.9 x 15.4 cm, list of ship's battle stars, list of commanding officers. PNAM.

Essex (CV 9)

82 *U.S.S. Essex CV–9*. Cover: Saga of the Essex. Anon. Baton Rouge: Army & Navy Pictorial Publishers, 1946. 168 pp., blue hardcover with embossed title and embossed gold wing, 30.8 x 23.3 cm, photos, ports., map. Dornbusch 1950: 884, Smith: 7259, Zeigler: 2578. NDL, PNAM.

Euryale (AS 22)

83 *Epic of the U.S.S. Euryale Submarine Tender (AS–22)* (cover). Anon. N.p., [1946?]. Photograph of AS–22 and dark printing on cover, photos, ports., map. NDL, SFL (both photocopies).

Eversoll (DD 789)

84 *U.S.S. Eversoll* (cover). Anon. Tacoma, Wash.: Marland Bookcraft, 1946. 6 leaves, 22 x 28 cm, photos, ports. Dornbusch 1950: 885, Smith: 7260. No known copy location.

Fall River (CA 131)

85 [Cruise Book of the USS *Fall River*]. Anon. Erie, Pa: Advance Printing & Lithographing Co., 1945. 56 leaves, 28 cm, photos, ports. Dornbusch 1950: 886, Smith: 7268. No known copy location.

Fanshaw Bay (CVE 70)

86 *Straddled: U.S.S. Fanshaw Bay*. Cover: Straddled: A Short History of the U.S.S. Fanshaw Bay. Anon. Seattle: Seattle Printing & Publishing Co., [1946?]. 72 pp., gray-green hardcover with blue printing and silhouette of *Fanshaw Bay*, 27.3 x 20.8 cm, photos, ports., map. Dornbusch 1950: 887. NDL.

Farenholt (DD 491)

87 *Saga of the Fighting "F" U.S.S. Farenholt (DD 491), Flagship of DesRon Twelve.* Anon. N.p., [1946?]. 56 pp., blue hardcover with black printing and silhouette of DD 491, 28 x 22 cm, photos, ports., large folded map tipped in, crew roster, award roster. Dornbusch 1950: 888, Smith: 7273. NDL.

Fogg (DE 57)

88 *Our Ship's Log, July 7th, 1943 to October 7th, 1945.* Cover: U.S.S. Fogg (DE 57), 1945. Doyle L. Riley, ed. Philadelphia: C. E. Howe & Co., 1945. 20 leaves, silver softcover with blue printing and emblem, 21.5 x 28 cm, photos, ports. Dornbusch 1950: 889, Smith: 7731, NDL.

Foote (DD 511)

89 *Shipmates: The Crewbook, U.S.S. Foote DD 511—"45".* Cover: U.S.S. Foote, 1942–1945. Anon. New York: Robert W. Kelly Publishing Corp., [1945?]. 71 pp., blue hardcover with gold printing and decoration, 27.3 x 20.3 cm, photos, ports., map, roster. Dornbusch 1950: 890, Smith: 7283. NYPL.

Foss (DE 59)

90 *U.S.S. Foss DE–59, Second Anniversary (July 23, 1943–July 23, 1945).* Anon. N.p.: Tropical Press Printers, 1945. 14 leaves, 17.5 x 26 cm, photos, ports. Dornbusch 1951 supp.: 1473, Smith: 7288. NDL.

Franklin (CV 13)

91 *Big Ben, the Flattop: The Story of the U.S.S. Franklin.* Lt. Marvin K. Bowman, ed. Atlanta: Albert Love Enterprises, [1946?]. 68 leaves, blue and buff hardcover with blue and buff printing and silhouette of CV 13 in background, 30.9 x 23.2 cm, photos, ports., roster. Dornbusch 1950: 891, Smith: 7292. Private collection.

Fulton (AS 11)

92 *The Fulton Bow Plane, Anniversary Edition.* (cover, which is also page one). Lt. G. C. Westlund, ed. Printed on board September 12, 1942. 10 leaves, printed on one side only, white paper cover, 27.4 x 20.3 cm, photos, drawings, outline of AS 11 activity during the year. SFL. This is an enlarged anniversary edition of the ship's newspaper and is not a typical cruise book.

93 *The Fulton Bow Plane, Second Anniversary.* (cover, which is also page one). Lt. E. W. Ross, ed. Printed on board September 12, 1943. 18 leaves, printed on one side only, white paper cover, 27.4 x 20.3 cm, photos, drawings, outline of ship's activities during the year. SFL. This is an enlarged anniversary edition of the ship's newspaper and is not a typical cruise book.

94 *The Fulton Bow Plane, Third Anniversary.* (cover, which is also page one). Lt. A. C. De Blanc, ed. Printed on board September 12, 1944. 34 leaves, printed on one side only, white paper cover, 27.4 x 20.3 cm, photos, drawings, outline of ship's activities during the year. SFL. This is an enlarged anniversary edition of the ship's newspaper and is not a typical cruise book.

Gallup (PF 47)

95 *U.S.S. Gallup (PF–47) List of Officers & Crew Sailing From San Pedro, Wednesday, May 31, 1944 to Australia, New Guinea, Leyte Gulf, the Aleutians, and Dildo Key.* Cover: U.S.S. Gallup PF–47, List of Officers and Crew, Corrected November 1949, United States Coast Guard. Anon. New York: Benj. H. Tyrrel, [1949?]. 8 leaves, gray paper cover, 17.6 x 12.6 cm, roster. NYPL.

General A. E. Anderson (AP 111)

96 *The Log of the Mighty "A", 1943–1945—Being the Story in Words and Pictures of the Wanderings of the U.S.S. General A. E. Anderson.* Cover: The Mighty "A", 1943—1945. Anon. N.p., [1945?]. 50 leaves, blue hardcover with gold printing and embossed silhouette of AP 111, 31 x 23.4 cm, photos, ports., map, roster. Dornbusch 1950: 892, Smith: 7303. NDL, USNA (rebound).

General H. S. Hodges (AP 144)

97 *Supplement to Former Album* (on page 1). Anon. N.p., May 1941. 6 leaves, no cover, 21.1 x 27.8 cm, photos, ports., map, roster. Private collection.

98 *U.S.S. General H. S. Hodges (AP 144), 1945.* Cover: U.S.S. General H. S. Hodges (AP 144). Anon. N.p., [1946?]. 24 leaves, dark blue hardcover with gold printing, 22 x 28.4 cm, photos, ports., roster. Private collection.

General Leroy Eltinge (AP 154)

99 *Log of the U.S.S. General Leroy Eltinge AP–154.* Cover: Log of the U.S.S. Leroy Eltinge. Anon. Seattle: Farwest Printing Co., [1946?]. 24 leaves, blue hardcover with gold printing and silhouette of AP 154, 27 x 20.5 cm, photos, ports., map, roster. Dornbusch 1950: 893, Smith: 7304. USNA.

General M. L. Hersey (AP 148)

100 *U.S.S. General M. L. Hersey (AP 148)* (cover). Anon. N.p., [1946?]. 32 pp., gray and blue hardcover with photo of AP 148, 29.3 x 21.6 cm, photos, map. Private collection.

General O. H. Ernst (AP 133)

101 *U.S.S. General O. H. Ernst (AP 133), First Year of Service, 15 July 1944 to 15 July 1945* (cover). Anon. N.p., [1946?]. 12 leaves, white paper cover with photo of AP 133 and blue printing, 27.9 x 21.6 cm, photos. Private collection.

General R. E. Callan (AP 139)

102 *Callan Cruises, Aug. '44–June '46.* Lt. Comdr. A. H. Roberts, MC, ed. N.p., [1946?]. 101 pp., blue hardcover with gold printing and embossed silver and gold emblem, 28.5 x 21 cm, photos, ports., map. Dornbusch 1951 supp.: 1475, Smith: 7306. NDL, NYPL (film).

General R. L. Howze (AP 134)

103 *U.S.S. General R. L. Howze AP–134.* Lt.(jg) Ottis H. Abrey, USCG. N.p., [1946?]. 32 leaves, blue embossed hardcover with gold printing and emblem, 27.3 x 20.3 cm, photos, ports., roster, chronology of each voyage. USCGA.

General R. M. Blatchford (AP 153)

104 *The Story of the U.S.S. Gen. R. Blatchford (AP–153): An Illustrated Account of the Career of the U.S.S. General R. M. Blatchford (AP–153) From Keel Laying to the End of the Last War—Time Voyage.* Anon. Seattle, Wash.: Deers Press, [1946?]. 16 leaves, 26.5 cm, photos, ports. Dornbusch 1951 supp.: 1474. NDL.

General S. D. Sturges (AP 137)

105 *U.S.S. General S. D. Sturges, Pacific Year 1944–1945.* Cover: Pacific Year. Lt. Comdr. R. L. Geiger et al., eds. N.p., [1946?]. 88 pp., blue hardcover with gold printing and anchor, 27.7 x 20.3 cm, photos, ports., map, roster. Dornbusch 1950: 896, Smith: 7307. NDL.

General W. A. Mann (AP 112)

106 *U.S.S. General W. A. Mann AP–112.* Anon. Portland, Oreg.: T. G. Merkley Co., [1946?]. 51 leaves, printed on one side only, blue hardcover with gold printing and silhouette of AP 112, loose-leaf binding, 23 x 28 cm, photos, ports., map, roster. Dornbusch 1950: 894, Smith: 7308. NDL.

General W. C. Langfitt (AP 151)

107 *Our Sentimental Journey, November 23–December 10, 1945.* Anon. Berkeley: Lederer Street & Zeus, 1946. 32 pp. Smith: 7309. No known copy location.

General W. H. Gordon (AP 117)

108 *The U.S.S. General W. H. Gordon: A Photo-Story of Duty Aboard Navy Troop Transport AP–117 Manned by the United States Coast Guard.* Cover: The U.S.S. General W. H. Gordon. Lt. (jg) Robert N. Aylin, USCGR. N.p., 1945. 112 leaves, dust jacket with photo of ship, blue hardcover with silver printing, 23.5 x 29.8 cm, photos, ports. Dornbusch 1951: 1476, Smith: 7077, Zeigler: 2273. USCGA, USCGPA, USNA (rebound).

General William Mitchell (AP 114)

109 *Ship's Album, U.S.S. General William Mitchell AP–114.* Anon. Portland, Oreg.: T. G. Merkley Co., [1946?]. 24 leaves, 23 x 29 cm, photos, Dornbusch 1950: 895, Smith: 7310. No known copy location.

George F. Elliott (AP 105)

110 *The Fighting Fox* (cover). Anon. Seattle: Sterling Engraving Co., [1946?]. 35 leaves, tan hardcover with brown printing and drawing of fox, 28 x 20.7 cm, photos, ports., map. Dornbusch 1950: 897, Smith: 7311. Private collection.

George W. Ingram (DE 62) and (APD 43)

111 *The Cruise of the G. W. Ingram, 1943–1945.* Cover: The Cruise of the USS Geo. W. Ingram DE 62–APD 43. Lt. John Ohnysty, USNR, ed. N.p., [1946?]. 40 pp., blue softcover with title printed in black and white silhouette of DE 62, spiral binding, 19.1 x 25.4 cm, photos, ports., map, roster, photos of conversion to APD. NDL.

Gilbert Islands (CVE 107)

112 Philadelphia: Campus Publishing Co. Advertised in *All Hands,* November 1946. No known copy location.

Gilmer (DD 233) and (APD 11)

113 *War Diary of USS Gilmer.* Grahame F. Shrader. Lynnwood, Wash.: Edmonds Printing Co., 1987. 17 pp., white and gray paper cover, 28 x 21.6 cm, photos. Private collection. This is an atypical booklet published over forty years after World War II and not a true cruise book. It is included because of its similarity to cruise books.

Goodhue (APA 107)

114 *First Year of the U.S.S. Goodhue APA 107, November 11, 1944–November 11, 1945.* Anon. Los Angeles: W. F. Lewis, [1945?]. 35 leaves, 21 x 26 cm, photos, map. Dornbusch 1951 supp.: 1477. NYPL.

Goshen (APA 108)

115 *The Register, U.S.S. Goshen.* Anon. N.p., [1946?]. 36 leaves, 28 cm, photos, ports. Dornbusch 1950: 898, Smith: 7328. No known copy location.

Guadalcanal (CVE 60)

116 *U.S.S. Guadalcanal: Memory Log* (cover). Anon. N.p., [1946?]. 46 pp., embossed blue hardcover with gold printing and photo of *Guadalcanal,* 21.4 x 26.5 cm, photos, ports., map. Dornbusch 1950: 899, Smith: 7350. NDL, SMPH, USNA.

Guam (CB 2)

117 *U.S.S. Guam: Her Story, 1944–1945.* Cover: U.S.S. Guam. Comdr. Walter A. Mahler, ChC, ed. N.p., [1946?]. 50 leaves, embossed blue hardcover with gold printing and silhouette of *Guam,* 36.4 x 27.4 cm, photos, ports., map, roster. Dornbusch 1950: 900, Smith: 7351. NDL.

Hamlin (AV 15)

118 *U.S.S. Hamlin, Department of the Navy* (cover). Ens. J. P. LeBlanc, USNR, ed. Birmingham, Ala.: Alabama Engraving Co., [1945?]. 51 pp., blue hardcover with green title and decoration, 26.2 x 31.2 cm, photos, ports., map, roster. NDL.

Hancock (CV 19)

119 *The "Fighting Hannah": A War History of the U.S.S. Hancock CV–19.* Cover: The Fighting Hannah: U.S.S. Hancock CV 19. E. G. Hines, USNR. Seattle: Sterling Engraving Co., [1946?]. 72 leaves, blue hardcover with gold printing and silhouette of CV 19, 28 x 21 cm, photos, ports., map. Dornbusch 1950: 901, Smith: 7406a, Zeigler: 2605. NDL, PNAM, USNA. Reprinted by the Battery Press, Nashville, Tenn. in 1969.

Harris (APA 2)

120 *This Is the Story of the U.S.S. Harris APA–2 in World War II.* Cover: Four Years Afloat PA–2. Lt (jg.) L. E. Wright, USNR, ed. Boston: Rand Press, [1946?]. 50 leaves, embossed blue-green hardcover with gold printing and silhouette of PA 2, 28.4 x 22.2 cm, photos, ports., map. NDL, private collection.

Harry Lee (APA 10)

121 *History of the Harry Lee, 1940–1945.* Anon. N.p., [1945?]. 12 leaves, 28 cm, photos, ports. Dornbusch 1950: 902, Smith: 7387, NDL.

Haven (AH 12)

122 Not a WW II cruise book, but a mimeographed 19-page history of 1945–1953 operations, including the Korean War. NDL.

Heermann (DD 532)

123 *War History of the U.S.S. Heermann.* Cover: Destroyer X, U.S.S. Heermann DD–532. Anon. San Angelo, Tex.: Newsfoto Publishing Co., March 1947. 30 leaves, embossed blue hardcover with white printing, 27.5 x 20.5 cm, photos, maps, roster, award list. USNA.

Henry A. Wiley (DM 29)

124 *USS Henry A. Wiley DM 29 Scrapbook*. Cover: USS Henry A. Wiley DM 29. Lt. L. B. Varney, USNR, ed. Fowler, Ind.: Benton Review Publishing Co., [1946?]. 74 pp., blue hardcover with gold printing and silhouette of DM 29, 27.4 x 20.3 cm, photos, ports., map. Dornbusch 1950: 904, Smith: 7395. NDL, USNA.

Herald of the Morning (AP 173)

125 *The U.S.S. Herald of the Morning*. Cover: U.S.S. Herald of the Morning. Anon. Seattle: Sterling Engraving Co., [1946?]. 18 leaves, white hardcover with blue printing and ship silhouettes, 28 x 20.6 cm, photos, ports., map. Dornbusch 1950: 905, Smith: 7396. Private collection.

Heywood L. Edwards (DD 663)

126 *War Diary of the U.S.S. H. L. Edwards*. Cover: U.S.S. H. L. Edwards. Anon. Seattle: F. McCaffrey, [1946?]. 20 leaves, blue hardcover with gold printing and decoration, 27 x 20.5 cm, photos, ports., map, roster, award list. Dornbusch 1950: 906, Smith: 7390. NYPL, USNA.

Highlands (APA 119)

127 *The Story of U.S.S. Highlands*. Don L. Oeschlaager and S. W. Tuell. N.p., 1946. 35 pp., 23 cm, photos. Dornbusch 1951 supp.: 1478. No known copy location.

Hoggatt Bay (CVE 75)

128 *U.S.S. Hoggatt Bay, Queen of the CVEs*. Cover: CVE–75: The Story of the U.S.S. Hoggatt Bay. Anon. San Angelo, Tex.: Newsfoto Publishing Co. (not noted in NYPL copy), [1946?]. 60 leaves, embossed blue hardcover with black printing and silhouette of CVE 75, 20.5 x 27.4 cm, photos, ports., roster. Dornbusch 1950: 907, Smith: 9410. NYPL, USNA (rebound).

Hollandia (CVE 97)

129 *"Old 97": The Story of the U.S.S. Hollandia*. Lt. Arthur C. Walsh. San Diego: Arts & Crafts Press, December 1945. 63 leaves, embossed blue hardcover with gold printing, 31 x 23.5 cm, photos, ports., maps, roster. Dornbusch 1950: 908, Smith: 7413. NDL, NYPL, PNAM, USNA.

Hornet (CV 12)

130 *The United States Ship Hornet: First War Cruise, 1943–1945* (cover). Anon. Printed on board October 1945. 24 leaves, green paper cover with black printing and silhouette of *Hornet,* 26.5 x 20.9 cm, photos, ports., map. Dornbusch 1950: 909. NDL, NYPL, TIL.

131 *The Tale of the . . . Hornet* (cover and top of page 1). Stanley Blumenthal. N.p., [1945?]. 27 pp., blue paper cover with black printing and view of *Hornet,* 29.2 x 22.4 cm. Private collection, PNAM (variant containing additional 16-page roster of the crew).

Houston (CA 30)

132 Listed in NDL for CA 30. Author did not see this book, and it more likely describes the successor CL or a prewar cruise book for CA 30.

Huntington (CL 107)

133 *Cruise of the USS Huntington (CL107): June to 8 December 1948.* Cover: USS Huntington 107. Ens. Charles F. Rauch, ed. Baltimore, Md.: Horn-Shafer Company, [1949]. Blue hardcover with silver embossed lettering. 45 leaves, photos, map on end leaves. NDL. This is the first cruise book for *Huntington,* built under the wartime construction program and commissioned soon after the end of WW II.

Hutchins (DD 476)

134 *U.S.S. Hutchins (DD 476): "The Spirit of 476."* Anon. N.p., [1945?]. 28 pp., 26 x 20 cm, photos, ports. Dornbusch 1950: 910, Smith: 7441. NDL (rebound).

Idaho (BB 42)

135 *U.S.S. Idaho BB 42: Mighty I, Commissioned March 1919.* Cover: U.S.S. Idaho. Lt.(jg) E. L. Collings, ed. N.p., [1946?]. 24 leaves, embossed green hardcover with bow view of BB 42, 27.3 x 20.5 cm, photos, ports., map. NSP, private collection.

Indiana (BB 58)

136 *U.S.S. Indiana Battleship.* Cover: U.S.S. Indiana. Anon. Berkeley: Lederer Street & Zeus Co., [1945?]. 151 pp., blue and white hardcover with embossed title and decoration, 27.5 x 20.5 cm, photos, ports., crew roster. Dornbusch 1950: 911, Smith: 7445. NDL, NWC, USNA (rebound).

Intrepid (CV 11)

137 *U.S.S. Intrepid.* Cover: The Intrepid. Anon. Los Angeles: Metropolitan Engravers, [1946?]. 168 pp., embossed white hardcover, 28.5 x 22 cm, photos, ports. Dornbusch 1950: 912, Smith: 7448. NDL, PMAN, SMPH, USNA.

138 *History of U.S.S. Intrepid.* 2 vols. Vol. 1, *16 August 1943–1 March 1945*, 49 pp. Vol. 2, *1 March 1945–1 June 1945*, 12 pp. Anon. N.p., 1945. Hardcover (rebound mimeograph) 26.3 x 20 cm. NDL. This is an operational history originally classified confidential.

Izard (DD 589)

139 *War Record of the U.S.S. Izard (DD 589), 1943–1945* (cover and top of page 1). Anon. N.p., [1946?]. 13 pp., paper cover with cross-hatched gray background, 23.5 x 15.6 cm. Private collection.

Jason (ARH 1)

140 *U.S.S. Jason in World War II* (cover). Anon. N.p., [1945?]. 113 pp., manila paper cover, 28 x 21.6 cm, photos, ports., map, roster. Dornbusch 1950: 913, Smith: 7467. NDL (rebound).

John Q. Roberts (APD 94)

141 *The Story of the U.S.S. John Q. Roberts APD 94, Commissioned 8 March 1945*. Cover: U.S.S. John Q. Roberts APD 94. Anon. Jacksonville: Douglas Printing Co., [1946?]. 14 leaves, blue hardcover with gold printing and anchor emblem, 28 x 20.4 cm, photos, ports., map, roster. Advertised in *All Hands* July 1947. NDL.

Karnes (APA 175)

142 *The Mighty "K": U.S.S. Karnes APA 175* (cover). Anon. N.p., [1946?]. 18 leaves, soft, heavy blue paper cover with blue printing and red and blue decoration, 18.3 x 26.8 cm, photos, ports., map. NDL.

Kenneth Whiting (AV 14)

143 *Photographed, Edited, and Published Aboard the Kenneth Whiting AV–14, 1944–1945*. Cover: Life Aboard the Kenneth Whiting. Anon. Printed on board [1946?]. 25 leaves, soft cover with photo of *Whiting* and red printing on red background, 26 x 20.7 cm, photos, ports. Private collection.

Kenton (APA 122)

144 *The Mighty "K": Photographic History of the U.S.S. Kenton and Its Personnel* (cover). Anon. N.p., [1946?]. 22 leaves, softcover with blue and white printing and photo of Kenton in background, 27 x 34 cm, photos, ports., map, officer roster. NDL.

Kershaw (APA 176)

145 *Log of U.S.S. Kershaw APA 176.* Anon. N.p., [1946?]. 32 pp., photos, ship's history. This citation was taken from NDL card file although copy could not be located in NDL. No other known reference.

Kwajalein (CVE 98)

146 *Kwaja-Lines: First Anniversary, USS Kwajalein CVE 98, June 7 '44–June 7 '45* (cover). Anon. Printed on board 1945. 16 pp., softcover, 23.5 x 15.9 cm, photos. Private collection.

147 *The U.S.S. Kwajalein CVE 98: 100,000 Miles Under the Keel During World War II* (cover). Anon. Printed on board [1945?]. 5 pp., paper cover, 28 x 21.6 cm. Private collection.

Lake Champlain (CV 39)

148 *Farewell to the Great Lake: USS Lake Champlain, the Anniversary and Inactivation Issue* (cover). Anon. New York: Anchor Printing, [1947?]. 16 leaves, paper cover, 27 x 20.5 cm, photos, list of plank owners. Dornbusch 1950: 919, Smith: 7486. USNA (rebound).

Lander (APA 178)

149 *USS Lander, 1945* (cover). Ens. B. K. Isaacs, Jr., USNR, ed. N.p., [1946?]. 57 leaves, embossed blue hardcover with title and shield printed in gold, 20 x 24.5 cm, photos, ports., map, roster. Dornbusch 1950: 920, Smith: 7489. NDL, NWC, NYPL, USNA.

Lanier (APA 125)

150 *Sea Goin' Memories: U.S.S. Lanier U.S. Navy Attack Transport APA 125, 22 December 1944–1 November 1945.* Anon. N.p., [1946?]. 112 pp., heavy blue paper cover printed in dark blue, red, and yellow, spiral binding, 30.5 x 23 cm, photos, port., map, roster. Dornbusch 1950: 921, Smith: 7497. NDL, USNA.

LaSalle (AP 102)

151 *U.S.S. LaSalle Family Album.* Cover: U.S.S. LaSalle. SoM3c D. L. Moore, ed. Seattle: Metropolitan Press, [1946?]. 31 pp., light blue paper cover with dark blue printing and photo of ship, 26.2 x 20.3 cm, photos, ports., roster. NDL.

LCI 542

152 *History of U.S.S. LCI 542, 1943–1945.* Frederick R. Van Vechten, Jr., USNR, (inactive). [New York: C.P. Young Co., 1946?]. 36 pp., gray paper cover with black printing, 23.5 x 15.6 cm, photos, roster. NDL.

Leary (DD 879)

153 Copy in Navy Department Library. Author has not seen and has no details. No other reference.

Lejeune (AP 74)

154 *USS Lejeune (AP–74).* Anon. Tacoma, Wash.: M. D. Boland, [1947?]. 9 leaves, 22 x 28 cm, photos, ports. Dornbusch 1950: 922, Smith: 7504. NDL.

Lenoir (AKA 74)

155 *War History, USS Lenoir AKA 74, December 31, 1944 to November 4, 1945.* Lt. D. O. Grossman, USNR. N.p., 1945. 20 leaves, printed on one side only, 33 cm, roster. Dornbusch 1950: 923, Smith: 7507. NYPL (film). This is a typewritten manuscript, probably reproduced by mimeograph.

Lexington (CV 16)

156 *Tarawa to Tokyo, 1943–46.* Lt. (jg) C. R. Million and Lt. (jg) S. E. Whicher, eds. [Los Angeles: Standard Lithographic Co.], 1945. 83 leaves, blue hardcover with gold printing, 28.3 x 21.7 cm, photos, ports., map on endsheets and loose maps, 48.2 x 63.8 cm map of the Pacific Theater, roster. Dornbusch 1950: 926, Smith: 7522. NSP, PNAM, USNA.

157 *The Blue Ghost: A Photographic Log and Personal Narrative of the U.S.S. Lexington in Combat Operation.* Capt. Edward Steichen, USNR (Ret.). New York: Harcourt Brace and Co., 1947. 149 pp., blue hardcover, photos, ports. Dornbusch 1950: 925, Smith: 7817, Zeigler: 2690. NDL, private collection.

Leyte (CV 32)

158 *Shakedown Cruise United States Ship Leyte CV–32, August–December 1946.* Cover: U.S.S. Leyte CV32. Lt. Comdr. O. E. Sporrer, USN, ed. Atlanta: Albert Love Enterprises (publisher), Foot & Davies (printer), [1947?]. 100 leaves, embossed blue hardcover with gold printing, 31 x 23 cm, photos, ports., map. USNA. This is the first cruise book for this World War II-constructed ship commissioned soon after the war.

Little Rock (CL 92)

159 *The "Arkansas Traveler": U.S.S. Little Rock, 1945–1947.* Ens. C. L. Beach, ed. New York: Paramount Printing & Publishing Co., 1947. 32 leaves, blue hardcover with gold printing and silhouette of *Little Rock,* 28.5 x 21.7 cm, photos, ports., map, roster. Advertised in *All Hands* February 1948. NDL, private collection. This is the first cruise book for this World War II-constructed ship commissioned in June 1945.

Louisville (CA 28)

160 *Lady Lou.* Cover: 1944. Anon. N.p., 1944. 16 leaves, blue hardcover with silhouette of CA 38 and gold printing, spiral binding, 22.2 x 28.3 cm, photos, ports., map. NSP.

161 *Man of War: Log of the United States Heavy Cruiser Louisville.* Cover: Man of War. Anon. Philadelphia: Dunlap Printing Co., 1946. 219 pp., embossed brown hardcover with gold printing and silhouette of *Louisville,* 31.3 x 23.3 cm, photos, ports., map. Dornbusch 1950: 927, Smith: 7534, Zeigler: 2631. NDL, NSP, NWC.

Lowry (DD 770)

162 *United States Ship Lowry (DD–770): Leyte, Mindoro, Lingayen, Iwo Jima, Tokyo Raid, Okinawa, Occupation of Japan.* Cover: Lowry Scrap Book, 1944–45. Anon. N.p., [1947?]. 41 leaves, blue hardcover with white printing, 27.5 x 21 cm, photos, ports., maps. Dornbusch 1950: 928, Smith: 7536. NDL, NWC, USNA..

LSM 267

163 *The Cruise of The LSM 267* (cover). Robert P. Langlangs and staff. Elmira, N.Y.: Quality Printers, [1946?]. 32 pp., orange hardcover with black printing, 28 x 20.5 cm, photos, ports., map. NDL (photocopy).

LST 471

164 *The United States Ship Landing Ship Tank 471.* Cover: The Fightin' 471. Anon. Charleston: Walker, Evans & Cogswell, [1946?]. 10 leaves, blue hardcover with black printing and silhouette of LST, 28.3 x 21.9 cm, photos, ports., large folding map tipped in. Dornbusch 1950: 915, Smith: 7484. NDL, NYPL.

LST 491

165 *The Ol' Double Trouble.* Cover: The Ol' Double Trouble USS LST 491. Lt. James W. Knox, USNR. Pittsburgh: R. T. Lewis Co., 1949. 56 pp., blue and white hardcover with blue printing and drawing of *LST 491*, 22.2 x 14.5 cm, photos, ports., map. Dornbusch 1950: 916, Smith: 7482. Private collection.

LST 511

166 *Turn To: USS LST 511, United States Atlantic Fleet Amphibious Force.* Cover: USS LST 511, Turn To'. Anon. N.p., December 1945. 10 leaves, blue softcover with silver printing, 23.4 x 15.7 cm, photos, ports., roster. NDL.

LST 530

167 *Log of the LST 530.* Cover: Log of the LST 530. Lt. Comdr. Anthony D. Duke, Commanding. Lt. Comdr. Anthony Drexel Duke, ed. New York: Phillip Andrews Publishing Co., 1945. 16 leaves, blue hardcover with gold printing and spiral binding, 23.5 x 31 cm, photos, ports., map. Dornbusch 1950: 917, Smith: 7243. NDL.

LST 533

168 *United States Ship Landing Ship Tanks 533: Ship History (December 1943 to April 1953)* (cover). Lt. E. C. Ross, USNR. N.p., [1953?]. 15 pp., yellow paper cover with photo of *LST 533*, stapled binding, 26.5 x 20.2 cm, photos, ports. USNA.

LST 692

169 *The Flatbottom U.S.S. LST 692* (cover). Anon. N.p., [1945?]. 14 leaves, blue, yellow, and gray softcover with black printing and photo of ship, 26 x 20.5 cm, photos, map. Dornbusch 1950: 918, Smith: 7485. NDL.

LST 925

170 *A Little Bit of Nonsense.* Cover: LST 925. Anon. N.p., [1946?]. 26 pp., buff softcover with blue printing, 23.2 x 15.3 cm, photos, ports., roster. NDL.

Ludlow (DD 438)

171 *U.S.S. Ludlow (DD 438): "She's Been Around".* Anon. N.p., 1946. 36 pp., plus 6 unnumbered pp., blue softcover with dark blue printing, 27.7 x 21.9 cm, photos. Dornbusch 1950: 929, Smith: 7538. NDL.

Lunga Point (CVE 94)

172 *U.S.S. Lunga Point CVE 94: A Pictorial Log Covering the Ship's Career in the War Against the Axis, 14 May 1944–14 May 1945.* Cover: U.S.S. Lunga Point, Department of the Navy, 14 May 1944 to 14 May 1945. Lt. S. Linton Smith, USNR, ed. Raleigh, N.C.: Edwards & Broughton Co., [1945?]. 240 pp., maroon hardcover with gold printing and embossed emblem, 31.2 x 23.3 cm, photos, ports., map. Dornbusch 1950: 930, Smith: 7803. NDL, NYPL, PNAM, TIL.

Macomb (DD 458) and (DMS 23)

173 *History of the U.S.S. Macomb DD 458–DMS 23, September 1941–September 1945.* Cover: U.S.S. Macomb, 1941–1945. Anon. Baltimore: Horn-Shafer Co., [1945?]. 82 pp., blue hardcover with gold printing and silhouette of DD 458, 27.2 x 19.9 cm, photos, ports., map, roster. Dornbusch 1950: 931, Smith: 7543. NDL, NYPL.

Madison (DD 425)

174 *The Unofficial Story of the Destroyer USS Madison.* Cover: There Was A Ship. Anon. [Philadelphia: George H. Buchanan Co., 1945?]. 16 leaves, buff paper cover with black title and reproduction of watercolor painting of DD 425, 25.4 x 19.4 cm, one photo, drawings. Dornbusch 1950: 932, Smith: 7560. NDL, NYPL (film).

Makassar Strait (CVE 91)

175 *U.S.S. Makassar Strait on Her Maiden Crossing of the Equator on 14 October 1944 in World War II.* Anon. N.p., October 1944. 37 pp., blue-gray softcover, 20 x 26.3 cm, photos, ports., partial roster. NDL (missing cover).

176 *U.S.S. Makassar Strait.* Cover: The Mighty Mac' (CVE–91). Anon. Seattle: Sterling Engraving Co., [1946?]. 36 leaves, red hardcover with title and decoration printed in silver, 27 x 20.5 cm, photos, ports., map. Dornbusch 1950: 933, Smith: 7562. NDL, NYPL, USNA.

Makin Island (CVE 93)

177 *The Escort Carriers in Action: The Story—In Pictures—of the Escort Carrier Force, U.S. Pacific Fleet* (cover). *Supplement for U.S.S. Makin Island (CVE–93).* Comdr. Price Gilbert, Jr., USNR. Atlanta: Ruralist Press, 1946. 184 pp. plus *Makin Island* supplement of 43 pp., blue hardcover with gold printing, 31.1 x 23.5 cm, photos, ports., map, roster. NDL, NSP, USNA. See Naval Aviation section for the version of this book on escort carrier operations without the *Makin Island* supplement.

Marcus Island (CVE 77)

178 *U.S.S. Marcus Island CVE 77.* Cover: U.S.S. Marcus Island. Lt. (jg) D. G. Lannamann, USNR, et al. eds. San Diego: Arts & Craft Press, [1946?]. 48 leaves, blue flexible cover with gold printing and silhouette of CVE 77, 31 x 23.5 cm, photos, ports., roster. Private collection.

Marquette (AKA 95)

179 *The Long Way Home or We've Been Around: Being a Chronicle of the First Cruise of the U.S.S. Marquette from New York, New York on 1 July 1945 to Norfolk, Virginia on 19 April 1946.* Cover: The Long Way Home: U.S.S. Marquette. K. W. Vining, CY. Norfolk: Eugene L. Graves, June 1946. 73 pp., gray hardcover with gold-embossed shield and red printing, 23.6 x 15.9 cm, photos, ports., map, roster. Dornbusch 1950: 934, Smith: 7567. NDL.

Maryland (BB 46)

180 *U.S.S. Maryland 1941–1945* (cover). Anon. Baton Rouge: Army & Navy Pictorial Publishers, 1946. 51 pp., blue hardcover with embossed title and gold Navy seal, 27.2 x 19.6 cm, photos, ports., map. Dornbusch 1950: 935, Smith: 7572. NDL, NWC, USNA.

Massachusetts (BB 59)

181 *A Pictorial History of the U.S.S. Massachusetts.* Cover: U.S.S. Massachusetts, April 1942–August 1945. Anon. [San Antonio, Tex.: Universal, 1945?]. 126 pp., embossed blue hardcover with title and *Massachusetts* silhouette in silver, 28.6 x 22.3 cm, photos, ports., map. Dornbusch 1950: 936, Smith: 7574. MSL, NDL, NSP, NWC, NYPL, USNA.

Mayflower (WPE 183)

182 *U.S.S. Mayflower*. Edwin A. Falk. New York: Benj. H. Tyrrel, [1946?]. 71 pp., blue hardcover with gold printing, 24 x 16 cm, photos, USNA.

Mayo (DD 422)

183 *War Cruise, USS Mayo*. Anon. N.p., [1946?]. 55 pp., 22 x 28 cm, photos, ports., map. Dornbusch 1950: 937, Smith: 7575. NDL.

McNair (DD 679)

184 *History of the U.S.S. McNair, Commissioned December 30, 1943*. Cover: U.S.S. McNair (DD 679). Anon. San Francisco: Haywood H. Hunt, February 1946. 24 leaves, blue softcover with dark blue printing and silhouette of DD 679, 26 x 17.5 cm, photos, ports., roster. NDL.

Meade (DD 602)

185 *The Album of USS Meade*. Cover: USS Meade. Lt. (jg) Harry Greenspan, ed. N.p., [1945?]. 72 leaves, embossed blue hardcover with embossed ship silhouette, 27.2 x 21 cm, photos, ports., 48.7 x 44 cm map folded in pocket in back of book. Dornbusch 1950: 938, Smith: 7343, NDL.

Mellena (AKA 32)

186 *Mellena Days (AKA 32)* (cover). Anon. Portland, Oreg.: T. G. Merkley Co., [1945?]. 47 leaves, 29 cm, photos, ports., map. Dornbusch 1950: 939, Smith: 7580. No known copy location.

Melvin (DD 680)

187 *Story of U.S.S. Melvin, Commissioned November 24, 1943*. Cover: This Is Our Story. Anon. San Francisco: Heywood H. Hunt, 1945. 43 pp., photos, ports., roster. Dornbusch 1950: 940, Smith: 7581. NDL, NSP, NYPL (film).

Memphis (CL 13)

188 *U.S.S. Memphis CL 13, 1942–1945* (cover). Lt. Walter O. Severson USNR, ed. N.p., [1946?]. 12 leaves, blue softcover with dark blue printing and photo of CL 13 in background, 29.8 x 22.5 cm, photos, ports. Dornbusch 1950: 941, Smith: 7582. NDL.

Meriwether (APA 203)

189 *The Mighty "M"*. Cover: U.S.S. Meriwether APA 203, 1944–45. Lt. (jg) Clark F. Woodard, ed. N.p., [1946?]. 60 leaves, blue hardcover with gold printing and shield, 28.6 x 22.2 cm, photos, ports., roster. Dornbusch 1950: 942, Smith: 7584. NDL.

Miami (CL 89)

190 *The Story of the United States Ship Miami (CL89)*. Cover: U.S.S. Miami. Anon. Baton Rouge: Army & Navy Pictorial Publishers, 1946. 47 leaves, embossed blue hardcover with gold printing and silhouette of cruiser, 31 x 23 cm, photos, ports., map. Dornbusch 1950: 943, Smith: 7585. NDL, USNA.

Minneapolis (CA 36)

191 *The "Minnie" or The War Cruise of the U.S.S. Minneapolis*. A. T. Luey and H. P. Bruvold. Elkhart, Ind.: Bell Printing Co., 1946. 126 pp., blue hardcover with gold printing, 22.7 x 15.7 cm, photos, map, roster. Dornbusch 1950: 944, Smith: 7539, Zeigler: 2633. NDL, NYPL, TIL, USNA. This cruise book was reprinted about 1987 and contains some extra material not in the original 1946 printing.

Mississippi (BB 23)

192 *USS Mississippi: War Record, 1941–1945*. Cover: USS Mississippi, 1941–1945. Anon. Baltimore and New York: Thomsen–Ellis–Hutton Co., [1946?]. 126 pp., black hardcover with gold printing and silhouette of bow view of BB 23, 31 x 23 cm, photos, ports. Dornbusch 1950: 945, Smith: 7593. NDL, NYPL, USNA.

193 *U.S.S. Mississippi 1945*. Anon. N.p., 1945. 14 leaves, gray and green softcover with black printing and photo of BB 23, 26.9 x 21 cm, photos, ports. NDL.

Missouri (BB 63)

194 *The History of U.S.S. Missouri*. Cover: USS Missouri. Anon. Atlanta: Albert Love Enterprises, [1945?]. 59 leaves, blue hardcover with embossed title and gold-embossed reproduction of surrender plaque, 31 x 23 cm, photos, ports. Dornbusch 1950: 946, Smith: 7594. NDL, NYPL, TIL, USNA, WCL.

Mobile (CL 63)

195 *The Story of a Ship: USS Mobile and the Men Who Fought Her*. Cover: USS Mobile (CL 63). Anon. Long Beach: Greens, 1945. 80 leaves, blue hardcover with gold printing and silhouette of CL 63, 21 x 26 cm, photos, ports. Dornbusch 1950: 947, Smith: 7598. NDL, NYPL, USNA.

196 *The Mighty Mo*. Cover: CL 63. Anon. N.p., [1946?]. 50 leaves, blue hardcover with gold printing, 16.7 x 24.6 cm, photos, ports. NDL, USNA.

Monterey (CVL 26)

197 "History of the U.S.S. Monterey, 17 June 1943 to 2 September 1945." Anon. Unpublished typescript in three parts. Part I: Chronology; Part II: Narrative. Part III: Appendices. Various pagings. 26.5 x 19 cm. NDL (rebound in blue hardcover).

Montpelier (CL 57)

198 *War Diary of CL 57, U.S.S. Montpelier, September 1942–December 1945*. Cover: "Mighty Monty." Lt. J. B. Cralle, USNR, and Ens. J. R. Chadwick, USNR, eds. [New York: Robert E. Kelly Publishing Co.], December 1945. 39 leaves, blue hardcover with gold printing and photo of *Montpelier* pasted on, 20.3 x 26.7 cm, photos, ports., roster. Dornbusch 1950: 948, Smith: 7604. NWC, NYPL, USNA.

Montrose (APA 212)

199 *The 212* (cover). Anon. Mare Island, Calif.: Autumn 1945. 31 leaves, green paper cover with black printing, 26.4 x 20.3 cm, photos, ports., map, roster. NYPL.

Mount McKinley (AGC 7)

200 *First Cruise of the "Mighty Mac" USS Mount McKinley, 1944–1945*. Cover: First Cruise of the "Mighty Mac". Anon. N.p., [1945?]. 24 leaves, gray and white softcover with white printing, 28 x 21.6 cm, photos, ports. Dornbusch 1950: 949, Smith: 7613. NDL.

201 *Second Cruise of the "Mighty Mac" USS Mount McKinley: Occupation of Japan, September–November 1945*. Anon. N.p., 1945. 12 leaves, softcover, 27.4 x 20.5 cm. Smith: 7614. NDL.

202 *Third Cruise of the Mighty Mac: Far Eastern Commission, December 1945–February 1946*. Anon. N.p., 1946. 12 leaves, softcover, 27.4 x 20.5 cm. NDL.

203 *Fourth Cruise of the "Mighty Mac": Operation Crossroads*. Anon. N.p., [1946?]. 22 leaves, softcover, 27.4 x 20.5 cm. NDL.

Mount Vernon (AP 22)

204 *United States Ship Mount Vernon, a Navy Transport*. Cover: U.S.S. Mount Vernon. Anon. Philadelphia: Campus Publishing Co., 1946. 52 leaves, blue hardcover with gold-embossed printing, 27.5 x 20.3 cm, photos, ports., loose 25.3 x 70.8 cm map. Dornbusch 1950: 950, Smith: 7615. NDL, private collection.

Mountrail (APA 213)

205 *U.S.S. Mountrail APA 213: November 16, 1944 to December 1, 1945*. Cover: U.S.S. Mountrail APA 213. Anon. N.p., [1946?]. 38 pp., blue hardcover with gold printing, 28.4 x 22.1 cm, photos, ports., map, roster. Dornbusch 1950: 951, Smith: 7616. NDL, private collection.

Napa (APA 157)

206 *Napalogue*. Anon. Berkeley: Lederer Street & Zeus Co., 1946. 107 pp., blue hardcover with gold printing and ship in background, 27.5 x 20.5 cm, photos, ports., map, roster. Dornbusch 1950: 952, Smith: 7619, Zeigler: 2651. MSL, NDL, USNA.

Nashville (CL 43)

207 *Your Ship, the Nashville, 1942–45*. Cover: U.S.S. Nashville. Anon. N.p., [1946?]. 124 pp., blue hardcover with gold printing, 12.3 x 17.2 cm, photos, map. Dornbusch 1950: 953, Smith: 7620. NDL.

Natoma Bay (CVE 62)

208 "History of U.S.S. Natoma Bay (CVE–62), October 1945." Anon. N.p., n.d. 54 pp. NDL. This is a typed manuscript and was stamped "Confidential" when originally issued. It is an official operational report, not a cruise book.

Neshoba (APA 216)

209 *The History of the U.S.S. Neshoba.* Cover: U.S.S. Neshoba. Anon. San Angelo, Tex.: Newsfoto Publishing Co., [1946?]. 58 leaves, embossed blue hardcover with title and silhouette of APA 216, 20.5 x 27 cm, photos, ports., map, roster. Dornbusch 1950: 954, Smith: 7631. NDL, NYPL, USNA.

Nevada (BB 36)

210 *USS Nevada, 1916–1946.* Cover: USS Nevada. Lt. (jg) W. S. Wyatt, USNR, ed. San Francisco: James H. Barry Co., [1946?]. 196 pp., brown hardcover with gold printing and silhouette of *Nevada,* 31 x 23.7 cm, photos, ports., map. Dornbusch 1950: 955, Smith: 7632. NDL, private collection.

New Jersey (BB 62)

211 *War Log, USS New Jersey, 1943–1945.* Cover: War Log, USS New Jersey. Anon. N.p., [1946?]. 96 pp., gray and blue hardcover with blue printing and gray silhouette of *New Jersey,* 27.5 x 20.4 cm, photos, ports., map, officers roster. Dornbusch 1950: 956, Smith: 7634. NDL, NYPL, USNA.

New Kent (APA 217)

212 *U.S.S. New Kent APA 217* (cover). Anon. N.p., [1946?]. 20 leaves, 28 cm, photos. Dornbusch 1950: 957, Smith: 7635. NDL.

New Orleans (CA 32)

213 *The No Boat: The Unfinished Story of the U.S.S. New Orleans.* Lt. Clyde Carters, Jr. Berkeley: James J. Gillick & Co., [1945?]. 14 leaves, 22 x 14 cm, photos. Dornbusch 1950: 958, Smith: 7179. NDL (rebound), NYPL (film).

New York (BB 34)

214 *The History of the U.S.S. New York BB–34.* Cover: USS New York BB 34. Anon. San Angelo, Tex.: Newsfoto Publishing Co., [1947?]. 112 leaves, embossed blue hardcover with white printing and silhouette of BB 34, 20.5 x 27 cm, photos, ports., map, roster. USNA.

Nicholas (DD 449)

215 *U.S.S. Nicholas (DD 449) Destroyer.* Cover: U.S.S. Nicholas. Anon. Rochester, New York: Cohber Press, 1946. 55 pp., blue hardcover with gold printing and silhouette of DD 449, 28.5 x 21.5 cm, photos, ports., roster. Dornbusch 1950: 959, Smith: 7641. NYPL, USNA.

Nitro (AE 2)

216 *USS Nitro: A Chronological Story of the Cruise, April 44 to August 45* (cover). Anon. N.p., [1945?]. 9 leaves, white paper cover with drawing of ship and title printed in black, 23 x 20.5 cm, drawings, map, roster. NDL.

Noble (APA 218)

217 *The Story of a Good Ship: U.S.S. Noble (APA 218), 1944–1945.* Cover: U.S.S. Noble (APA 218). Anon. N.p., [1947?]. 42 pp., blue hardcover with gold-embossed title, 28 x 20 cm, photos, ports., map, roster, chronology of Pacific service. Dornbusch 1950: 960, Smith: 7642. NDL, NYPL, USNA.

North Carolina (BB 55)

218 *The Showboat: BB 55 U.S.S. North Carolina.* Cover: The Showboat. Anon. N.p., [1946?]. 72 leaves, blue hardcover with gold background for printing, 27.8 x 21.3 cm, photos, ports., map, roster. Dornbusch 1950: 961, Smith: 7649. NDL, NYPL NWC, USNA.

Oberon (AKA 14)

219 *War Diary of the U.S.S. Oberon.* Anon. Seattle: Frank McCaffrey Co., [1945?]. 16 leaves, 24 cm, photos, ports. Dornbusch 1950: 963, Smith: 7653. NDL.

Oconto (APA 187)

220 *Cruise Book: USS Oconto APA–187, 1944–46* (cover). Anon. Portland, Oreg: T. G. Merkley, [1946?]. 56 leaves, blue hardcover with title and silhouette of APA 187 printed in gold, 22 x 28 cm, photos, ports., map, roster. Dornbusch 1950: 964, Smith: 7654. NDL, USNA.

Oglethorpe (AKA 100)

221 *Log of U.S.S. Oglethorpe.* Anon. Seattle: Sterling Engraving Co., [1946?]. 27 leaves, 19 x 26 cm, photos, ports. Dornbusch 1950: 965, Smith: 7657. NDL.

Okaloosa (APA 219)

222 *U.S.S. Okaloosa (APA–219)* (cover). Anon. Tacoma, Wash.: Johnson Cox Co., [1945?]. 6 leaves, buff softcover with black printing and photo of ship, spiral binding, 22 x 28 cm, photos, ports., roster. Dornbusch 1950: 966, Smith: 7658. NDL, NYPL.

Oklahoma City (CL 91)

223 *The Yearling: A Pictorial History of the First Year in the Life of the United States Ship Oklahoma City, December 1944–December 1945.* Cover: U.S.S. Oklahoma City. Anon. Rochester, N.Y.: DuBois Press, [1946?]. 185 pp., blue hardcover with gold-embossed printing and Indian shield, 27.5 x 20.5 cm, photos, ports., map, roster. Dornbusch 1951 supp.: 1482, Smith: 7659. NDL, NYPL, USNA.

Otus (AS 20)

224 *The Story of the USS Otus.* Cover: Otus Odyssey. Chaplain E. I. Van Antwerp, USNR, ed. N.p., [1946?]. 47 leaves, blue hardcover with silver printing and emblem, 27.3 x 20 cm, photos, ports., roster. Private collection.

Panamint (AGC 13)

225 *The U.S.S. Panamint: Amphibious Force Flagship 13, Her Voyage and Her Mission, World War II.* Anon. N.p., [1945?]. 36 leaves, photos. Dabney Catalogue 352: 445. No known copy location.

226 *Panamint Parade of the Bikini Bums.* Cover: Panamint Parade. Anon. N.p., 1946. 44 leaves, blue hardcover with gold printing, 26.7 x 21 cm, photos, port, map, passenger list. Private collection. This is a post-WW II book covering the Bikini atomic bomb tests shortly after the close of WW II.

Pasadena (CL 65)

227 *CL–65 U.S.S. Pasadena* (cover). Anon. San Angelo, Tex.: Newsfoto Publishing Co., [1945?]. 38 leaves, 20 x 27 cm, photos, ports., map, roster. Dornbusch 1950: 967, Smith: 7675. NDL.

Pelias (AS 14)

228 *Saga of the U.S.S. Pelias Submarine Tender (AS–14).* Anon. San Francisco: Schwabacher-Frey Co., 1946. 24 leaves, heavy buff paper cover with blue printing and photograph of AS 14, 30.5 x 22.9 cm, photos, ports. NDL (photocopy), SFM.

Pennsylvania (BB 38)

229 *War History of the U.S.S. Pennsylvania (BB 38)*. Cover: War History of the USS Pennsylvania. Lt. Clifton Cates, Jr. Published by Ship's Welfare Fund. Seattle: Metropolitan Press, [1946?]. 66 pp., heavy blue paper cover with black printing and silhouette of BB 38, spiral binding, 30.5 x 23 cm, photos, ports., maps, list of dead. Dornbusch 1950: 968, Smith: 7182. NDL, NWC, NYPL, USNA.

Pensacola (CA 24)

230 *USS Pensacola CA–24, 1929 thru 1946*. Cover: U.S.S. Pensacola. Anon. San Francisco: Phillips & Van Orden Co., 1946. 108 pp., blue hardcover with gold printing and silhouette of *Pensacola*, 28.5 x 22 cm, photos, ports., map, roster. Dornbusch 1950: 969, Smith: 7682, Zeigler: 2660. NDL, NWC, NYPL, USNA.

Phelps (DD 360)

231 *History of USS Phelps (DD 360), 1936–1945*. Cover: USS Phelps DD 360 History. Lt. Roger E. Jones, USN (Ret.), ed. N.p., [1946?]. 345 pp., white softcover with red and black printing and picture of *Phelps* with dates 1936–1945 and motto in English and Latin, 21.6 x 28 cm. NWC.

Philippine Sea (CV 47)

232 *The Story of the U.S.S. Philippine Sea (CV–47)*. Cover: The U.S.S. Philippine Sea, 1946–1948. Anon. N.p., [1948?]. 56 leaves, blue hardcover with gold printing and embossed silhouette of CV 47, 31.2 x 23.6 cm, photos, ports., map. NDL, PNAM, USNA. Part of wartime construction, CV 47 was commissioned shortly after WW II ended. This is the first cruise book for CV 47.

Pickens (APA 190)

233 *The Story of the Pickens APA 190, September 1944–April 1946*. Anon. N.p., [1946?]. 23 pp. Smith: 7688. No known copy location.

Pittsburgh (CA 72)

234 *Unofficial Log of the USS Pittsburgh: Boston–Panama–Jamaica–Miami–New York, Twelfth of January to Twentieth of January, 1945*. Cover: Over the Bounding Main. Anon. N.p., [1945?], flexible blue cover with black printing, spiral binding, 29.2 x 22.9 cm, photos, ports., drawings. NDL.

Pocomoke (AV 9)

235 *History of USS Pocomoke (AV–9) (Large Seaplane Tender), From 28 April 1941 to 2 September 1945* (cover). Anon. Printed on board November 1945. 55 pp., printed on one side of sheet only, buff softcover with black printing and photo of AV 9, 26.3 x 19.8 cm, photos, ports., map, chronology and history. NDL.

Pondera (APA 191)

236 *U.S.S. Pondera (APA–191)*. Cover: U.S.S. Pondera APA 191, 1944–46. Anon. San Diego: Frye & Smith, March 1946. 58 leaves, blue hardcover with gold printing and emblem, 28.6 x 22 cm, photos, ports., map, roster. Dornbusch 1950: 970, Smith: 7691, Zeigler: 2661. NDL, NYPL, USNA.

Quincy (CA 71)

237 *Odyssey of the U.S.S. Quincy*. Cover: Odyssey: U.S.S. Quincy. Lt. (jg) W. E. Jessup, ed. N.p., [1946?]. 111 pp., blue hardcover with gold printing and Navy Department seal, 28.7 x 22.3 cm, photos, ports., map, roster. Dornbusch 1950: 971, Smith: 7710. NDL, TIL, USNA.

Randolph (CV 15)

238 *The Gangway: A Pictorial History of the U.S.S. Randolph's First Year at Sea, October 9, 1944 to October 9, 1945*. Cover: U.S.S. Randolph. Lt. Jack Herod, ed. N.p., 1946. 80 leaves, maroon hardcover with embossed title and gold-embossed emblem, 31 x 23 cm, photos, ports., maps, roster. NDL, NSP, NYPL, USNA.

Razorback (SS 394)

239 *U.S.S. Razorback SS 394*. Lt. Aubrey, ed. N.p., [1945?]. 31 leaves, blue hardcover with gold printing and emblem, 30.8 x 23 cm, photos, ports., roster. Dornbusch 1950: 972, Smith: 7718. NDL, USNA.

Register (APD 92)

240 Advertised in *All Hands*, July 1947. No other reference.

Remey (DD 688)

241 *A Record of the Service of the U.S.S. Remey Consisting of Copies of Letters, Newspaper Clippings, and Photographs Regarding this Ship From Her Launching to the Close of World War II*. Assembled by Charles Mason Remey. Washington: Charles Mason Remey, [1947?]. 59 leaves, typed on one side of leaf only, flexible brown binder, 28 x 21.7 cm, photos, ports. NYPL. This is not a true cruise book, but a scrapbook and brief history of USS *Remey* put together by Charles Remey. Few copies were made; the NYPL copy is No. 5.

Reno (CL 96)

242 *U.S.S. Reno* (cover). Anon. San Francisco: Carlisle, [1945?]. 28 leaves, blue hardcover with title and decoration printed in gold, 28 x 21.2 cm, photos, ports., roster. NDL, USNA.

Renville (APA 227)

243 *The United States Ship Renville APA 227*. Cover: U.S.S. Renville. Ens. Oscar Lax, ed. N.p., January 1946. Blue softcover with title and eagle printed in gold, 22 x 14.5 cm, photos, ports., roster. NDL, USNA.

Richard P. Leary (DD 664)

244 *Log of the U.S.S. Richard P. Leary*. Anon. N.p., [1946?]. Unpaged, blue hardcover, 23.5 x 18 cm. USNA.

Richmond (CL 9)

245 *U.S.S. Richmond in the Pacific War*. Anon. Philadelphia: Allen Lane & Scott, December 1945. 10 leaves, heavy paper cover with printing in green and black and photo of CL 9, spiral binding, 28.5 x 22 cm, photos, ports., map, roster. Dornbusch 1950: 973, Smith: 7730. NDL, NYPL, USNA.

Ringgold (DD 500)

246 *The Officers and Men of the U.S.S. Ringgold Bid You a Cordial Welcome and Offer You This Booklet*. Anon. Printed on board October 1945. 14 pp. Smith: 7732. No known copy location. This is not a true cruise book, but a visitor's brochure.

Rodman (DMS 21)

247 *War History of the U.S.S. Rodman* (cover). Anon. N.p., [1946?]. 47 pp., buff paper cover with black printing and photo of DMS 21, 13.4 x 20 cm, photos, map, roster. NDL.

Sacramento (PG 19)

248 *"Homeward Bound"*. Cover: Cruise of the U.S.S. *Sacramento*. Lt. (jg) Sidney L. Erwin, ed. N.p., 1939. 52 pp. Gray-blue softcover, 27.5 x 21 cm, photos, ports., roster, map. NDL. This cruise book, which predates American involvement in WW II, describes a 1939 homeward cruise from the Orient to New York via Suez.

Saint Croix (APA 231)

249 *U.S.S. Saint Croix APA 231, 1944–1945*. Anon. Portland, Oreg.: T. G. Merkley Co., [1945?]. 48 pp., blue paper cover with gold printing and emblem, 28 x 21.7 cm, photos, ports., roster. Dornbusch 1950: 974, Smith: 7754. NDL.

St. Louis (CL 49)

250 *The Lucky Lou CL 49: The Saga of the Lucky Lou*. Anon. San Francisco: Allied Photographic, 1945. 61 leaves, blue hardcover with gold-embossed letters. Private collection.

Saint Paul (CA 73)

251 *The War Cruise of the U.S.S. Saint Paul*. Comdr. Thomas H. Suddath, USN, and Lt. Comdr. Stanley T. Dommer, USNR, eds. N.p., [1945?]. 96 pp., blue hardcover with title printed in gold, 28 x 18.5 cm, photos, ports., map, roster. Dornbusch 1950: 975, Smith: 7831. NDL, USNA.

Saipan (CVL 48)

252 *The First Hitch: A History of the First Year in the Life and Times of the United States Ship Saipan CVL–48 From July 1946 to July 1947*. Cover: U.S.S. Saipan 1946–1947. Chaplain Alden A. Read and CPhoM Cecil P. Free, eds. Philadelphia: Campus Publishing, [1947?]. 176 pp., blue hardcover with title and ship silhouette embossed in gold, 27 x 20 cm, photos, ports., map. NDL, USNA. This is the first cruise book of a ship built in the war program and completed shortly after WW II.

Salt Lake City (CA 25)

253 *The Story of the U.S.S. Salt Lake City, 1929 to 1946*. Cover: USS Salt Lake City. Anon. Long Beach: Green's, 1946. 72 pp., blue hardcover with gold printing, 23.6 x 16.3 cm, photos, ports., map, roster. Dornbusch 1950: 976, Smith: 7755. NDL, NSP.

Samuel N. Moore (DD 747)

254 *War Record, U.S.S. Samuel N. Moore, Destroyer Division 122.* Cover: U.S.S. Samuel N. Moore, Destroyer–747, 24 June 1944–15 August 1945, War Record Book. Lt. (jg) W. G. Solum, USNR, ed. YM2c William Robert Hoke, publisher, [1945?]. 27 pp., heavy paper cover with blue printing and photograph of ship, 27.2 x 20.6 cm, photos, map. NDL.

San Diego (CL 53)

255 *U.S.S. San Diego Cruiser.* Cover: U.S.S. San Diego, World War II. , Ens. Peter J. Firra, ed. Berkeley: Lederer Street & Zeus, [1946?]. 127 pp., blue hardcover with gold printing and silhouette of CL 53, 27.4 x 20.5 cm, photos, ports., map, roster. NDL, USNA.

San Francisco (CA 38)

256 *One Ship, U.S.S. San Francisco, The Crew's Cruise Book.* Cover: U.S.S. San Francisco, One Ship. Anon. San Francisco: Crocker Union Lithography Co., 1945. 41 leaves, blue and gray hardcover with silhouette of CA 38 and Golden Gate Bridge, 22.1 x 28.3 cm, photos, ports. Dornbusch 1950: 977, Smith: 7756. NDL, USNA (rebound).

San Jacinto (CVL 30)

257 *A Short History of the U.S.S. San Jacinto, 3 May 1944–14 September 1945.* Anon. San Francisco: Merrill Reed, [1945?]. 77 pp., blue hardcover with title printed in gold, 28 x 21.5 cm, photos, ports., map, roster, award roster. Dornbusch 1950: 978, Smith: 7757. NDL, USNA.

San Juan (CL 54)

258 *USS San Juan.* Cover: Panther Strikes USS San Juan. E. G. Hines, USNR. Seattle: Sterling Engraving Co. (not noted in NYPL copy), [1946?]. 53 leaves, cream hardcover with orange and black printing and logo, 28 x 20.9 cm, photos, ports., map. Dornbusch 1950: 979, Smith: 7405. NYPL, USNA (rebound).

San Saba (APA 232)

259 *The San Saba: U.S.S. San Saba (APA 232)* (cover). Anon. N.p., [1946?]. 16 leaves, gray paper cover with black printing, 20 x 28 cm, photos, ports., map. Dornbusch 1950: 980, Smith: 7758. NDL.

Sanborn (APA 193)

260 *U.S.S. Sanborn* (cover). Anon. Seattle: Sterling Engraving Co., [1946?]. 48 leaves, heavy blue paper cover with gold printing and silhouettes of ship, spiral binding, 27 x 21.2 cm, photos, ports., map, roster. Dornbusch 1950: 980A, Smith: 7759. NDL, NYPL.

Sangamon (CVE 26)

261 *The Story of the U.S.S. Sangamon: An Oil Can With Wings*. Cover: U.S.S. Sangamon. Anon. Baton Rouge: Army & Navy Pictorial Publishers, [1945?]. 64 leaves, blue hardcover with gold lettering and red and gold logo of flying oil can, 22.9 x 30.6 cm, photos, ports., map. Dornbusch 1950: 981, Smith: 7760. NDL, PNAM.

Santa Fe (CL 60)

262 *The U.S.S. Santa Fe: A Pictorial Record of a Light Cruiser During the War Years, 1942–1945*. Cover: U.S.S. Santa Fe CL–60. Lt. (jg) Forrest W. Voss and Ens. Lewis A. Kremer, eds. Chicago: Rogers Printing Co., [1946?]. 169 pp., blue hardcover with gold-embossed title and emblem, 31.1 x 23.4 cm, photos, ports., map. Dornbusch 1950: 982, Smith: 7947. NDL, PNAM, USNA.

Saratoga (CV 3)

263 *Sara: The Story of the U.S.S. Saratoga*. Lt. B. J. Richards, ed. N.p., [1946?]. 173 pp., blue hardcover with gold printing and silhouette of CV 3, 23.5 x 30.5 cm, photos, ports., 55.8 x 74.2 cm map inserted loosely. Dornbusch 1950: 983, Smith: 7761, Zeigler: 2671. NDL, PNAM, USNA (rebound).

Saufley (DD 465)

264 *U.S.S. Saufley (DD 465): Her Story* (cover). Anon. Charleston: Walker, Evans & Cogswell, [1946?]. 53 pp., orange softcover with black printing and silhouette of destroyer, 17.6 x 12.5 cm, photos, ports., roster. Dornbusch 1950: 984, Smith: 7762. NDL.

Savo Island (CVE 78)

265 *Battle Baby: A Pictorial History of the Escort Carrier USS Savo Island (CVE 78)*. Cover: 125,000 Miles of Pacific Hell and History: A Pictorial History of the Escort Carrier U.S.S. Savo Island (CVE 78). Lt. Brantford B. Benton, ed. Baton Rouge: Army & Navy Publishing Co., 1946. 132 pp., embossed blue hardcover with gold printing, 30.8 x 23.3 cm, photos, ports., map, roster. Dornbusch 1950: 985, Smith: 7763, Zeigler: 2675. NDL.

Seahorse (SS 304)

266 *Logbook of the Second War Patrol*. 140 pp., Beachcomber Books, Cortaro, Arizona, Catalogue of November 1985. No known copy location. Author has not seen this book and there is a question as to whether it is a cruise book.

Shamrock Bay (CVE 84)

267 *"The Mighty Rock": The Story of the USS Shamrock Bay CVE 84*. Cover: USS Shamrock Bay CVE 84. Anon. Baton Rouge: Army & Navy Pictorial Publishers, 1946. 95 pp., green hardcover with gold printing and decoration, 27 x 19.5 cm, photos, ports., map. Dabney Catalogue 324, November 1988. Private collection.

Shangri-la (CV 38)

268 *Shangri-la to Bikini*. E. G. Hines. N.p., [1946?]. 127 pp., blue hardcover with embossed title, 27.4 x 20.3 cm, photos, ports., map. Dornbusch 1950: 987, Smith: 7406. NDL.

Shannon (DM 25)

269 *Saga Shannon: The Story of the USS Shannon DM 25 in Action, 1944–1945*. Cover: Saga Shannon, 1944–1946: USS Shannon DM 25. John Noyes. New York: J. Curtis Blue, [1945?]. 80 pp., blue hardcover with gold printing and decoration of mine and chain, 31.2 x 23.3 cm, photos, ports., maps, roster. Dornbusch 1950: 988, Smith: 7652, Zeigler: 2655. NDL, NYPL.

Shea (DM 30)

270 *The Fighting Story of the Shootin' Shea: A Complete Review of the U.S.S. Shea DM 30 and the Thrilling Part She and Her Valiant Crew Played in Bringing About Our Greatest Victory* (cover). James E. T. Carrigan, ed. New York: Collinson & Klingman, [1945?]. 48 pp., white paper cover with blue and red printing, 27.5 x 23 cm, photos, ports., map, roster. Dornbusch 1950: 989, Smith: 7780. NDL, NYPL.

Sheliak (AKA 62)

271 *U.S.S. Sheliak, Commissioned 1 Dec. 1944* (cover). George Downing, ed. San Francisco: Hooper Printing Co., [1946?]. 32 pp., hardcover with silver printing and photograph of AKA 62, 29.8 x 22.4 cm, photos, ports., map, roster. Private collection.

Siboney (CVE 112)

272 *Siboney News: Souvenir Edition, 14 May 1945–23 January 1946* (cover). Chaplain R. G. Massengale, ed. N.p., 1946. 6 leaves, paper cover with black printing and photograph of CVE 112, 15.3 x 22.9 cm, photos, ports., map. Private collection.

Sierra (AD 18)

273 *USS Sierra, Destroyer Tender, March 1944 to March 1946* (cover). Anon. N.p., [1946?]. 24 leaves, gray paper cover with black printing and silhouette of *Sierra*, 26.3 x 23.3 cm, photos, ports., map. NDL.

Sitkoh Bay (CVE 86)

274 *U.S.S. Sitkoh Bay CVE 86, 1945* (cover). Anon. N.p., [1945?]. 28 leaves, blue and white hardcover with printing in white and blue and bow view of CVE 86, 28 x 21.7 cm, photos, ports., map, roster. Dornbusch 1950: 991, Smith: 7796. NYPL.

Smith (DD 378)

275 *The Wartime Cruise of the U.S.S. Smith: DD 378* (cover). Anon. N.p., [1946?]. 48 pp., blue hardcover with title printed in gold, 28.5 x 22.2 cm, photos, ports., roster. Dabney Catalogue 372, March 1991. NDL, USNA.

Sperry (AS 12)

276 *A Pictorial Account of Crossin' the Line, U.S.S. Sperry (A.S. 12).* Cover: Crossin' the Line, 4 December 1945, U.S.S. Sperry (AS 12) Bound From Guam, Mariana Islands to Manus, Admiralty Islands. Comdr. F. M. Gambacorta et al., eds. N.p., 1945. 13 leaves, heavy white paper cover with blue printing and decoration and photograph of AS 12, 27.5 x 21.6 cm, photos, map, roster. NDL.

Springfield (CL 66)

277 *The Pictorial History of the USS Springfield CL–66*. Cover: USS Springfield. Anon. San Angelo, Tex.: Newsfoto Publishing Co., [1947?]. 62 leaves, blue hardcover with title and gold-embossed silhouette of ship, 20.5 x 27.4 cm, photos, ports., map, roster. Dornbusch 1950: 993, Smith: 7811. NDL, USNA.

Stevenson (DD 645)

278 *USS Stevenson (DD 645), 1942–1945*. Anon. Chicago: University Printing Co., [1946?]. 117 pp., blue hardcover with gold printing and silhouette of DD 645, spiral binding, 27.4 x 21 cm, photos, ports., map, roster. Dornbusch 1950: 994, Smith: 7818. NDL, NYPL, USNA (rebound).

Stewart (DD 224)

279 *"Ramp" 224* (cover). Anon. N.p., [1945?]. 8 pp., heavy blue paper cover with black printing and DD 224 in background, 26.8 x 20.3 cm, photos. Dornbusch 1950: 995, Smith: 7819. NDL, NYPL. This booklet describes the recommissioning of *Stewart* in the United States Navy after being captured by the Japanese in Java and spending most of WW II in the Japanese Navy.

Stormes (DD 780)

280 *U.S.S. Stormes DD 780*. Anon. N.p., [1945?]. 17 leaves, 28 cm, photos. Dornbusch 1950: 996, Smith: 7826. No known copy location.

Suwannee (CVE 27)

281 *War Log U.S.S. Suwannee CVE 27*. Anon. Baton Rouge: Army & Navy Pictorial Publishers, [1946?], end paper map printed by the Engineer Map Reproduction Plant. 86 pp., embossed blue hardcover, 27 x 19.4 cm, photos, map. Dornbusch 1950: 997, Smith: 7835. TIL.

Takanis Bay (CVE 89)

282 *U.S.S. Takanis Bay*. Cover: A Short History: U.S.S. Takanis Bay. Anon. Seattle: Sterling Engraving Co., [1946?]. 37 leaves, light blue-gray hardcover with black printing and silhouette of CVE 89, 27.4 x 21 cm, photos, ports. Dornbusch 1950: 997, Smith: 7841. NDL, NYPL, USNA.

Talamanca (AF 15)

283 *History of the USS Talamanca* (cover and top of page 1). Lt. (jg) Robert C. Alexander III, USNR. N.p., 1945. 10 pp., printed on one side, typewritten and mimeographed, paper cover with black printing and drawing of AF 15, 26.8 x 20.5 cm, roster. Private collection.

Tarawa (CV 40)

284 *U.S.S. Tarawa.* Anon. N.p., [1946?]. 32 leaves, blue softcover with gold printing and decoration, 26 x 19 cm, photos, ports., officer's roster. Dornbusch 1950: 998, Smith: 7847. NDL, USNA (rebound).

Tate (AKA 70)

285 *War-Time Log of the U.S.S. Tate AKA–70, 25 November 1944 to 12 December 1945.* Cover: War-Time Log of the U.S.S. Tate AKA–70. Anon. Everett, Wash.: Kane and Marcus Co., [1945?]. 20 leaves, blue hardcover with gold printing and silhouette of *Tate,* 26.2 x 20.9 cm, photos, ports., map, roster. Dornbusch 1950: 999, Smith: 7848. NDL, NYPL.

Taylor (DD 468)

286 *The U.S.S. Taylor DD–468, August 28, 1942–September 2, 1945.* Cover: U.S.S. Taylor. G. M. Holstein, ed. N.p., [1946?]. 48 leaves, blue hardcover with gold printing and anchor, 30.9 x 23.4 cm, photos, ports., map. Dabney Catalogue 380, December 1991. Private collection.

Tazewell (APA 209)

287 *Two-O-Nine: A Ship's Biography.* Cover: Two-O-Nine. HA1c Gilbert S. Mombach, ed. Published by USS *Tazewell* (APA 209). Berkeley: Howell-North Press, [1946?]. 96 pp., blue hardcover with gold printing, 27.2 x 20.3 cm, photos, ports., roster. Dabney Catalogue 380, December 1991. Private collection.

Tennessee (BB 43)

288 *USS Tennessee, December 7, 1941–December 7, 1945* (cover). Anon. Philadelphia: Clark Printing House, 1946. 209 pp., embossed blue hardcover with silver printing and silhouette of *Tennessee,* 31.2 x 23.4 cm, photos, ports., map, roster. Dornbusch 1950: 1000, Smith: 7849. NSP, NYPL, USNA.

Teton (AGC 14)

289 *U.S.S. Teton (AGC–14).* Cover: Teton Diary. Anon. Printed on board [1945?]. 24 leaves, 26.5 x 35 cm, photos, ports. Dornbusch 1951 supp.: 1486, Smith: 7852. NYPL (film).

Texas (BB 35)

290 *The United States Ship Texas in World War II: A Pictorial Review of the Accomplishments of the Thirty-One Year Old Battleship.* Cover: The United States Ship Texas in World War II. Anon. [New York: Publishers Print Co.], 1946 copyright by Welfare Fund, USS *Texas.* 63 leaves, blue softcover, 21 x 26 cm, photos. Dornbusch 1950: 1001, Smith: 7853, Zeigler: 2532. NSP, USNA (rebound).

Thadeus Parker (DE 369)

291 *U.S.S. Thadeus Parker DE–369, or Gullible's Travels.* Anon. N.p., [1945?]. 30 pp., 29 cm, photos, ports. Dornbusch 1950: 1002, Smith: 7854. NDL.

Theenim (AKA 63)

292 Log of the U.S.S. Theenim (AKA–63), December 23, 1944 . . . September 25, 1945. Anon. N.p., [1945?]. 12 leaves, blue softcover with gold printing and Coast Guard shield, 16 x 23.9 cm, photos, ports., roster. USCGPA.

Thetis Bay (CVE 90)

293 *U.S.S. Thetis Bay* (cover). Anon. N.p., [1945?]. 18 leaves, gray paper cover with black printing and drawing of CVE 90, 20 x 28 cm, photos, ports., map. Dornbusch 1950: 1003, Smith: 7855. NDL.

Thomas Jefferson (APA 30)

294 *In Oriental Waters: USS Thomas Jefferson (APA 30).* Cover: In Oriental Waters, USS Thomas Jefferson, July–November 1945. Lt. (jg) W. H. Rogers, ed. N.p., published by Ship's Welfare Department, 1945. 16 pp., heavy buff paper cover with brown printing and silhouette of APA 30, 27 x 20.5 cm, photos, ports. NDL.

295 *Pacific Islands Peoples and Crossing the Equator, USS Thomas Jefferson (APA 30).* Cover: A War Cruise of the Pacific, USS Thomas Jefferson, January 1945–July 1945. Anon. N.p., published by Ship's Welfare Department, 1945. 17 leaves, blue softcover with black printing, 26.7 x 20.4 cm, photos, ports., *Antheil Booksellers Catalogue,* July 1982. NDL.

Thorn (DD 647)

296 *USS Thorn DD 647: War Record and History, April 1943–March 1946*. Cover: USS Thorn DD 647. Anon. N.p., [1946?]. 53 pp., blue hardcover with printing in gold, 28.5 x 21.5 cm, photos, ports., map, list of plank owners. Dornbusch 1950: 1004, Smith: 7861. NDL, USNA.

Ticonderoga (CV 14)

297 *USS Ticonderoga War Log, 8 May 1944 to 5 October 1945*. Cover: USS Ticonderoga CV–14. Anon. Baton Rouge: Army & Navy Pictorial Publishers, 1946. 153 pp., embossed blue hardcover with gold printing, 31.3 x 23.3 cm, photos, ports., roster, map. Dornbusch 1950: 1005, Smith: 7864. No known copy location.

Topeka (CL 67)

298 *The U.S.S. Topeka CL 67: The Story of a Fighting Ship and Her Fighting Men, 1944–1945*. Cover: U.S.S. Topeka CL 67, 1944–1945. Ens. H. W. Arthur. Chaplain Mitchell T. Ancher, USNR, ed. Officers and men of the USS *Topeka*, publisher. N.p., [1946?]. 143 pp., blue hardcover with gold printing, 31 x 23.2 cm, photos, ports., roster. NDL.

Tulagi (CVE 72)

299 *U.S.S. Tulagi CVE–72, 1943–1946*. Anon. N.p., March 29, 1946. 34 pp., heavy blue paper cover, 20.3 x 26.7 cm, photos, ports., map. Private collection.

Tuscaloosa (CA 37)

300 *Tuscaloosa Merry-Go-Round, 1944* (cover). Anon. Philadelphia: E. A. Wright Co., [1945?]. Heavy gray paper cover with red and black printing and map and Indian in background, 21 x 25.5 cm, photos, ports. NDL.

Valley Forge (CV 45)

301 *U.S.S. Valley Forge World Cruise, 1947–48*. Comdr. J. P. Lunger, ed. N.p., [1948?]. 71 leaves, blue hardcover with gold printing and silhouette of CV 45, 31 x 23.6 cm, photos, ports., map. *Antheil Booksellers Catalogue*, January 1987. PNAM, USNA. This is the first cruise book of this ship built in the WW II shipbuilding program but completed after the war ended.

Velocity (AM 128)

302 Advertised in *All Hands*, July 1946. No known copy location.

Vicksburg (CL 86)

303 *U.S.S. Vicksburg (CL 86)* (cover). Anon. Long Beach, Calif.: Greens, [1946?]. 34 leaves, blue softcover with gold printing and silhouette of ship, 15.5 x 23 cm, photos, ports. Dornbusch 1950: 1006, Smith: 7944. NDL, USNA.

Vincennes (CA 44) and (CL 64)

304 *A Log of the Vincennes*. Donald H. Doris. Louisville: Standard Printing, 1947. 402 pp., 23.5 x 15.0 cm, photos, ports., casualty list. Advertised in *All Hands*, May 1948, Smith: 7240. USNA.

Vulcan (AR 5)

305 *Antheil Booksellers Catalogue*, October 1986. No known copy location.

Wakefield (AP 21)

306 *USS Wakefield AP–21, Operated for the U.S. Navy by the U.S. Coast Guard*. Cover: U.S.S. Wakefield AP–21 War Cruise History. Anon. Philadelphia: Clark Printing House, 1946. 66 pp., embossed blue hardcover with gold printing and Coast Guard seal and campaign ribbons, 27.6 x 20.4 cm, photos, ports., map. Advertised in *All Hands*, January 1948. NDL, USCGA.

Warren (APA 53)

307 *U.S.S. Warren*. Cover: The 53. W. J. Lugman, ed. Chicago: Suiter Craft, [1946?]. 48 leaves, embossed blue hardcover with white printing and star, 22.5 x 28 cm, photos, ports., map, roster. Smith: 7960. NDL, NYPL, USNA.

Wasatch (AGC 9)

308 *Cruise Book, USS Wasatch, 1944–45* (cover). Lt. (jg) James Conwell Welch, ed. Printed on board [1945?]. 25 leaves, paper cover with printing in purple and map of Pacific Ocean as background, 30 x 22.4 cm, photos, ports., map, roster. Dornbusch 1950: 1007, Smith: 7964. NDL.

Washington (BB 56)

309 *History of the U.S.S. Washington, 1941-1946.* Cover: U.S.S. Washington, 1941–1946. Lt. Comdr. R. W. Baker, ed. New York: Robert W. Kelly Publishing Corp., [1946?]. 119 pp., blue hardcover with title and emblem printed in gold, 27 x 20 cm, photos, ports. Dornbusch 1950: 1008, Smith: 7081, Zeigler: 2734. NDL, NWC, NYPL, USNA.

Wasp (CV 18)

310 *U.S.S. Wasp CV 18, (The Seventh Wasp Belonging to the United States), History (From Commissioning, 24 November 1943 to V–J Day, 2 September 1945, East Longitude Date.* Cover: U.S.S. Wasp CV 18, The Seventh Wasp, History, 24 November 1943–2 September 1945. Anon. N.p., 1945. 101 pp., typewritten on one side of page, heavy paper cover with white printing and photograph of CV 18 in background, 26.4 x 20 cm. NDL. This is not a true cruise book, but an operations history. It contains a chronology and narrative of operations of USS *Wasp* in WW II.

311 *Prep Charlie: A History of the Peregrinations of Our Fighting Lady, USS Wasp, While Mothering Air Group Eighty-one.* Cover: Prep Charlie. Anon. *Wasp* and Air Group 81, publisher. N.p., 1945. 208 pp., blue hardcover with gold printing and signal flags, 31 x 23 cm, photos, ports., map, roster of flight personnel. Dornbusch 1950: 1010, Smith: 7966, Zeigler: 2736. USNA.

312 *The Aircraft Carrier USS Wasp CV–18.* Cover: USS Wasp. Lt. James S. Ferris, ed. Boston: George F. Crosby Co., [1946?]. 107 pp., embossed blue hardcover with gold printing and decoration, 31.2 x 24 cm, photos, ports. Dornbusch 1950: 1009, Smith: 7965, Zeigler: 2735. Private collection.

Webster (ARV 2)

313 *U.S.S. Webster (ARV 2).* Cover: U.S.S. Webster: War Cruise to Tokyo Bay, 1945. Anon. N.p., [1946?]. 22 leaves, light blue softcover with dark blue printing, 23 x 15.4 cm, photos, ports., roster, chronology of ports of call. NDL.

Westmoreland (APA 104)

314 *United States Ship Westmoreland APA (AGCR) 104 . . . Flagship of Commander Transport Squadron Twenty-Two.* Cover: U.S.S. Westmoreland (APA 104). Anon. N.p., [1946?]. 12 leaves, blue softcover with gold printing and decoration, 27.2 x 19.8 cm, photos, ports., roster, chronology of travel. Dornbusch 1950: 1011, Smith: 7973. NDL.

West Point (AP 23)

315 *U.S.S. West Point: The Story of Naval Transportation and the Return of GI Joe.* Anon. Washington: 1945. 21 pp. Smith: 7889. No known copy location.

West Virginia (BB 48)

316 *USS West Virginia Crosses the Equator Again, October 1944.* Lt. R. O. Baumrucker, USNR, ed. San Francisco: Trade Pressroom, [1945?]. 78 pp., blue softcover with gold printing and Navy seal, 27.8 x 21.2 cm, photos, ports., roster. Controvich 1992. NDL, USNA.

Wichita (CA 45)

317 *300,000 Miles to Victory.* Cover: U.S.S. Wichita. Anon. N.p., [1946?]. 86 pp., blue hardcover with gold printing and eagle, 20.7 x 25.7 cm, photos, ports., map. Dornbusch 1950: 1012, Smith: 7984. NDL, NWC, USNA.

Wilkes-Barre (CL 103)

318 Advertised by Campus Publishing Co., Philadelphia, in *All Hands,* November 1946. No known copy location.

Wisconsin (BB 64)

319 *A Record of the USS Wisconsin BB64 Dedicated to Those Men of the United States Navy Who Served Aboard From 1943 to 1947.* Cover: USS Wisconsin. Anon. Philadelphia: Campus Publishing Co., [1947?]. 96 leaves, blue hardcover with gold printing and eagle, 29 cm, photos, ports. Dornbusch 1950: 1013, Smith: 7986. NYPL.

Wisteria USAHS

320 *Historical Report, 219th Hospital Ship Complement, USAHS Wisteria.* Anon. N.p., [1945?]. 24 pp., Smith: 7993. No known copy location. This is an Army ship and unit, but is included here because of its similarity to other material covered.

Woolsey (DD 437)

321 *U.S.S. Woolsey DD 437, Dedicated to the Men Who Manned and Fought the Woolsey World War II.* Cover: U.S.S. Woolsey DD 437. Anon. Philadelphia: Campus Publishing Co., [1946?]. 24 leaves, embossed blue hardcover with gold printing and decoration, 27.6 x 20.4 cm, photos, ports. Dornbusch 1950: 1014, Smith: 7998. NDL.

Yorktown (CV 10)

322 *Into the Wind: U.S.S. Yorktown in World War II CV 10* (cover). Lt. Robert L. Brandt, USNR, ed. N.p., 1946. 160 pp., embossed blue hardcover with gold printing and emblem, 31.4 x 23.5 cm, photos, ports., maps. Dornbusch 1950: 1015, Smith: 8004. NWC.

Yukon (AF 9)

323 *History of the U.S.S. Yukon (AF–9) Navy Supply Ship.* Comdr. A. L. McMullen and Y2c E. J. Roeckel. N.p., [1946?]. 125 pp., green paper cover with black printing and photo of AF 9, 28 x 22 cm, photos, ports., roster. Dornbusch 1950: 1016, Smith: 7556. NDL.

Zaurak (AK 117)

324 *Narrative War History of USS Zaurak (AK 117), March 17, 1944 to January 30, 1946.* Cover: History of the USS Zaurak (AK 117). Lt. (jg) T. H. Coley, USNR. N.p., 1946. 40 pp., roster. NSP (photocopy).

2

Naval Aviation Unit Books

Carrier Air Groups

Air Group 2

325 *Oriental Odyssey of Air Group Two.* Lt. (jg) Ken Nelson, ed. Chicago: Smith-Craft, [1946?]. 76 leaves, blue padded hardcover with gold-embossed title and silhouette of *Essex* class aircraft carrier, 30.5 x 22.9 cm, photos, ports., roster, reproduction of squadron insignia drawn by Walt Disney staff. PNAM.

Air Group 3

326 *Air Group 3* (cover). Anon. N.p., [1945?]. 14 leaves, 34 cm, photos, ports. Dornbusch 1950: 1040. No known copy location.

Air Group 6

327 *Carrier Air Group Six: A WW2 History of Carrier Air Group Six Prepared by the Officers & Men on the Last Cruise.* Cover: Air Group Six, United States Navy. Lt. Comdr. W. H. Fitzpatrick. N.p., [1945?]. 50 leaves, blue gray hardcover with title and four emblems, 31.5 x 23.1 cm, photos, ports., map, roster. PNAM.

Air Group 7

328 *Air Group Seven.* Lt. (jg) R. G. Hanecak, USNR, ed. N.p., [1945?]. 132 pp., embossed blue hardcover with red and gold printing and horseshoe, 28 x 36.3 cm, photos, ports., maps, roster. Dornbusch 1950: 1041. NYPL.

Air Group 9

329 *U.S.S. Essex, Carrier Air Group 9: The Record of the First Two Years, From the Forming of the Air Group in March 1942 to the Return From Action Against the Enemy in March 1944.* Anon. Chicago: Lakeside Press, [1945?]. 119 pp., 29 cm, photos, ports. Dornbusch 1950: 1043. Private collection.

330 *Air Group Nine Second Pacific Cruise, March 1944–July 1945, USS Lexington [and] USS Yorktown.* Anon. Allentown, Pa.: Miers-Bachman Lithographing Co., 1945. 88 leaves, 29 cm, photos, ports. Dornbusch 1950: 1042. No known copy location.

Air Group 10

331 *Carrier Air Group Ten, September 15, 1944–November 26, 1945, Aboard U.S.S. Intrepid, February 18, 1945–October 14, 1945*. Anon. Los Angeles: Metropolitan Engravers, 1946. 174 pp., 29 cm, photos, ports., roster. Dornbusch 1950: 1044, Dabney Catalogue, August 1991: 376. No known copy location.

Air Group 11

332 *Air Group Eleven: Fighting Squadron Eleven, "The Sundowners," August 9, 1943*. Anon. N.p., [1943?]. 14 leaves. Dornbusch 1950: 1051. No known copy location.

Air Group 17

333 *Air Group Seventeen Review, 1944–1945* (cover). Anon. Printed on board [1945?]. 14 leaves, heavy gray paper cover with black printing and photo of *Hornet* in background, 27 x 21 cm, photos, ports., map. NYPL.

Air Group 20

334 *Air Group 20: An Unofficial Portrayal of Carrier Air Group Twenty, U.S. Pacific Fleet, From Commissioning to Completion of Combat Cruise, 1943–1945*. Compiled from private and naval sources in 1949. Multiple authors. N.p., 1949. 84 pp., blue hardcover with gold printing and wings, 28.8 x 22.2 cm, photos, ports., roster, chronology of events. Dornbusch 1950: 1945, Zeigler: 1107. NDL.

Air Group 27

335 *The Log of Air Group Twenty-seven in World War II*. Anon. Chicago: Manz, [1945?]. 30 leaves, photos, ports. Dabney Catalogue, August 1991: 376. No known copy location.

Air Group 33

336 *The Odyssey of Thirty-three, May 1944–November 1945*. Cover: The Odyssey of Thirty-Three. Lt. (jg) Ralph H. Hallen, ed. N.p., [1946?]. 33 leaves, blue hardcover with gold printing, 27.4 x 20.6 cm, photos, ports., map, roster. NDL, PNAM.

Air Group 40

337 *Air Group 40, June 1944–August 1945* (cover). Anon. N.p., [1946?]. 50 pp., purple hardcover with blue printing and gold wings, spiral binding, 27.4 x 20.8 cm, photos, ports., roster. No known copy location.

Air Group 47

338 *There I Was: The Story of Air Group 47 on U.S.S. Bataan CVL–29, WW2*. Private collection list. No known copy location.

Air Group 60

339 *5,000 Miles Towards Tokyo*. Green Peyton. Norman, Okla.: University of Oklahoma Press, 1945. 173 pp., dust jacket, gray hardcover, 21 x 14.2 cm, reproductions of paintings by William F. Draper, map on end papers, roster. Private collection.

Air Group 81

340 See cruise book, *Prep Charlie* under *Wasp* (CV 18). It includes an account of Air Group 81.

Air Group 83

341 *Essex Air Group: CVG–83: The Combat Story of Air Group 83 and the U.S.S. Essex From 10 March 1945 to 13 September 1945*. Cover (on spine): Essex Air Group CVG 83. Anon. Chicago: Sleepeck-Helman Printing Co., January 1946. 127 leaves, blue hardcover with silhouette of *Essex* and white spine, 31.4 x 24.5 cm, photos, ports., roster. PNAM.

Air Group 86

342 *Carrier Air Group Eighty-six*. Robert Camp, Jr., ed. New York: North River Press, 1946. 140 leaves, white hardcover with blue, black, and gold printing and air battle scene as background, 31 x 23.6 cm, photos, ports., roster. Dornbusch 1950: 1046, Zeigler: 1416. NYPL.

Air Group 94

343 *Carrier Air Group Ninety-four, '44–'45*. Anon. N.p., [1948?]. 98 leaves, photos, ports., map, roster. Dabney Catalogue, August 1991: 376. No known copy location.

Air Squadrons

Bombing Squadron (VB) 1

344 *This Is It: The Story of Bombing Squadron One* (cover). J. W. Runyan. N.p., [1946?]. 33 pp., approximately 26.5 x 20.5 cm. PNAM (photocopy).

Bombing-Fighting Squadron (VBF) 1

345 *Bombing Fighting Squadron One, December 15, 1944 to November 1, 1945*. Cover: VBF 1. Anon. N.p., [1945?]. 63 leaves, blue hardcover with gold printing and wings and a head-on view of a Corsair, approximately 26.5 x 20 cm, photos, ports., roster. Private collection.

Fighting Squadron (VF) 1

346 *Fighting Squadron One: 1944 October 1945, Hi Hatters*. Cover: Fighting Squadron One: Hi Hatters. Lt. Comdr. Ralph G. Kelly, USNR. N.p., [1945?]. 72 leaves, white hardcover with black printing and high hat, 28.8 x 22.4 cm, photos, ports., map, roster. PNAM.

Fleet Air Photographic Squadron (VD) 1

347 *Introducing Fleet Air Photographic Squadron One (VD 1)*. Private collection list. No known copy location.

Meteorological Squadron (VPM) 1

348 *Ta Feng: A Story From Metron 1*. Anon. N.p., [1948?]. 17 leaves, yellow paper cover with black printing, 13.5 x 21 cm. Dornbusch 1951 supp.: 1498. NDL.

Torpedo Squadron (VT) 1

349 *Torpedo Squadron One, 1 October 1944–25 October 1945*. Anon. N.p., [1945?]. 16 leaves, blue-green softcover with silver printing, 28 x 22.2 cm, photos, ports., map, roster. Dornbusch 1950: 1047. NDL.

Air Transport Squadron (VR) 2

350 *The Martian Air Transport Squadron Two, Naval Air Station, Alameda, California, 1949*. Cover: The Martian VR 2. Anon. [Alameda, Calif.: Alameda Times Star Printing Co.], 1949. 28 leaves, blue hardcover with gold printing and decoration, 27.5 x 20.4 cm, photos, ports., map. NYPL, PNAM, TIL. This book covers the history of VR–2 through 1948.

Fighting Squadron (VF) 2

351 *Odyssey of Fighting Two*. Lt. Thomas L. Morrissey, USNR. Philadelphia: Lyon & Armor, 1945. 207 pp., embossed blue hardcover with gold shield, 27.5 x 20.3 cm, photos, ports., map. Dornbusch 1950: 1048. Private collection.

Photographic Interpretation Squadron 2

352 *Interpron Two: The Record of Our Squadron: How We Worked, Lived and Played While on Guam.* Cover: Interpron 2. Lt. William Corlett, ed. Lt. Richard B. Reinecker, publisher. Guam: August 1945. 141 pp., blue and buff paper cover with a tropical building and the number 2 printed in red, 28.3 x 22.5 cm, photos, ports., map. Dornbusch 1950: 1049. NDL.

Torpedo Squadron (VT) 2

353 *Scraps of Torpedo Two.* Lt. (jg) K. A. Nelson. N.p., [1945?]. 65 leaves, blue hardcover with gold printing and Avenger plane, spiral binding, 36.2 x 29.6 cm, photos, ports., map, roster. PNAM.

Air Transport Squadron (VR) 3

354 *Check Point 1944.* Cover: Check Point 1944: Annual Log Book of Air Transport Squadron Three. Lt. Bernard C. Capehart, Lt. Gerald W. Wickland, and Lt. John L. Springer, eds. N.p., 1944. 88 pp., blue hardcover with gold printing and decoration, 28.9 x 22.8 cm, photos, ports., map, roster. NDL, PNAM.

Composite Squadron (VC) 4

355 *The Deacon's Deamons—Composite Squadron 4, 2 September 1943 to 9 November 1944, U.S.S. Saginaw Bay CVE–82.* Private collection list. No known copy location.

Fighting Squadron (VF) 4

356 *Fighting Squadron Four: The Red Rippers, April 1944 to April 1945.* Cover: The Red Rippers (VF 4). Anon. N.p., [1945?]. Textured, tan hardcover with red and black printing and logo, 28.9 x 22.5 cm, photos, ports., roster. PNAM.

Fighting Squadron (VF) 5

357 *History of Fighting Squadron Five, February 1943 to May 1944.* (cover and top of page 1). Capt. Robert W. Duncan, USN (Ret.). N.p., n.d. 24 pp., white paper cover with black printing and logo, 28 x 21.5 cm. PNAM. This is not a true cruise book, but a historical account of the unit's operations written many years later, perhaps in the 1970s.

Fleet Air Photographic Squadron (VD) 5

358 *Meet VD 5*. Paul Orentlich, ed. J. Richmond Ritenour and Richard Reinecker, publishers. N.p.: VD5 Litho, May 20, 1945. 149 pp., tan and black paper cover with view of B–24 flying over island, 28 x 22.2 cm, photos, ports. Dornbusch 1950: 1050. NDL, PNAM.

Composite Squadron (VC) 6

359 *VC–6 War Time* (cover). Anon. N.p., [1946?]. 74 leaves, printed on one side only, flexible brown plastic cover with gold printing and logo, spiral binding, 22.3 x 27.5 cm, photos, ports., partial roster. PNAM.

Utility Squadron (VJ) 7

360 [UTRON 7 Pacific Log—Photo Log of VJ 7, July 1944–November 1945. No known copy location. Private collection list.]

Torpedo Squadron (VT) 9

361 *History of Torpedo Squadron Nine, 1944–45* (cover). Anon. [Burlington: Free Press, 1946]. 147 pp., light brown paper cover, 27.4 x 21 cm, photos. Controvich 1992. NDL (photocopy), private collection.

Patrol Squadron (VP) 12

362 *Black Cat Command* (cover). Andy Hewitt, ed. N.p., [1947?]. 11 leaves, black paper cover with orange printing and black cat logo, 32.3 x 23.5 cm, photos, ports., roster, diary of unit. NDL.

Utility Squadron (VJ) 13

363 *Utility Squadron 13: Odyssey, 1944–1945* (cover). Anon. San Diego: Frye & Smith, 1945. 48 leaves, blue hardcover with gold printing, 28.5 x 22.2 cm, photos, ports., map, roster. Dornbusch 1950: 1052. NDL.

Bombing-Fighting Squadron (VBF) 14

364 *The Kneepad of BombFightron–14* (cover). Lt. William B. Wilson, USNR. N.p., [1946?]. 64 pp., cream and black hardcover with cream printing and photo and logo, 27.3 x 20.3 cm, photos, ports., roster. PNAM.

BLIMPRON 14

365 *Overseas Mediterranean Operations, 1944, Blimpron 14.* Listed in holdings of library of the National Naval Aviation Museum, Pensacola, Florida, but author was unable to locate.

Bombing-Fighting Squadron (VBF) 17

366 *The Hellcat Squadrons of VF 17 VBF.* Anon. N.p., [1945?]. 20 pp., Controvich 1992. No known copy location.

Torpedo Squadron (VT) 17

367 *Torpedo Squadron Seventeen.* Anon. San Francisco: James H. Barry Co., [1945?]. 67 pp., 30 cm, photos, ports. Dornbusch 1951 supp.: 1502. No known copy location.

Fighting Squadron (VF) 18

368 *Fighting Squadron 18 (VF 18).* This citation was taken from NDL card file, although copy could not be located in NDL. No other reference known.

Composite Squadron (VC) 21

369 *Loose Ends.* John B. Patton, ed. N.p., [1945?]. 40 leaves, blue hardcover with gold printing, 28.8 x 22.2 cm, photos, ports., map, roster. PNAM.

Composite Squadron (VC) 27

370 *Saints: This Is the Story of VC–27 Composite Squadron, U.S.N., After Months of Operating as a Group in the Combat Zone of the Southwest Pacific.* Anon. N.p., [1946?]. 60 pp., 28 cm, photos, ports. Dornbusch 1950: 1054. No known copy location.

Fighting Squadron (VF) 31

371 *Fighting Squadron: A Veteran Squadron Leader's Firsthand Account of Carrier Combat With Task Force 58.* Robert A. Winston. New York: Holiday House, 1946. 182 pp. Controvich 1992. Private collection.

Fighting Squadron (VF) 46

372 *History of Fighting Squadron Forty-six: A Log in Narrative Form of Its Participation in World War II*. Hibben Ziesing. New York: Plantin Press, 1946. 43 pp., 26 cm, photos, maps. Dornbusch 1950: 1056. No known copy location.

Fighting Squadron (VF) 47

373 *There I Was: This Book Tells the Story of the Fighting Cocks of Fighting Forty-seven and the Liquidators of Torpedo Bombing Forty-seven*. Anon. Chicago: Smith, [1945?]. 40 leaves, photos. [March 1992?]: Dabney Catalogue 384. No known copy location.

Torpedo Bombing Squadron (VT) 47 (See entry 373.)

Composite Squadron (VC) 63

374 *Composite Squadron Sixty-three, August 1944–October 1945*. [Ens. Norman J. Anderson, ed.]. Baton Rouge: Army & Navy Pictorial Publishers, 1946. 47 leaves, 31 cm, photos, ports. Dornbusch 1950: 1059. No known copy location.

Patrol Squadron (VP) 63

375 *2nd Anniversary Along the Way*. Anon. N.p., [1945?]. 76 pp., blue softcover with black printing and gold logo, 30.5 x 22.8 cm, photos, ports., roster, awards roster. Dornbusch 1950: 1058. NDL.

Fighting Squadron (VF) 66

376 *Fighting 66*. Anon. N.p., [1946?]. 22 leaves, blue and white softcover with red printing and photo of banking Corsair, 27.8 x 21.2 cm, photos, ports., roster. PNAM.

Composite Squadron (VC) 70

377 *Travels of Composite Squadron Seventy*. Anon. Stevens Point: 1945. 103 pp. Dabney Catalogue 372, March 1991. No known copy location.

Fighting Squadron (VF) 77

378 *Fighting Squadron 77 (VF 77), 1945*. This citation was taken from the NDL card file although copy could not be located in NDL. No other known reference.

Patrol Squadron (VP) 81

379 *South Pacific, 1943–44, "Eighty-one" U.S.S. Patrol Squadron.* Cover: VP–81 Album. Anon. N.p., [1945?]. 102 pp., 22 x 29 cm, photos, ports. Dornbusch 1950: 1060. No known copy location. Dabney Catalogue, August 1991: 376 lists a book with the title *Patrol Squadron 81: "Black Cats," Nov. 25, 1943–July 15, 1944, 1944 Album.* This may be the same book or another book on VP–81.

Bombing Squadron (VB) 82

380 *Bombing Squadron 82.* Anon. N.p., [1946?]. 32 leaves, blue and white hardcover with clouds as background and white printing, 23.3 x 28.1 cm, photos, ports., map. PNAM.

Fighting Squadron (VF) 82

381 *Fighting Squadron Eighty-Two, 1945.* Lt. Armand Gordon Manson, ed. N.p., 1945. 34 leaves, brown hardcover with multicolor logo, 30.4 x 23.4 cm, photos, ports., roster. PNAM.

Bombing-Fighting Squadron (VBF) 83

382 *Bombing Fighting Eighty-three* (cover). A. C. Lefevre. N.p., [1946?]. 17 leaves, cover has the silhouette of a diving Corsair, 27 x 21 cm. PNAM (photocopy).

Fighting Squadron (VF) 83

383 *Fighting Squadron Eighty-Three* (cover). Anon. N.p., [1945?]. 53 pp., 26.6 x 20.7 cm, roster. PNAM (photocopy).

Composite Squadron (VC) 84

384 *The Chronicle of V.C. 84, 1944–1945.* N.p., [1945?]. 91 pp., photos, ports., map. Dabney Catalogue: August 1991 376. No known copy location.

Fighting Squadron (VF) 85

385 *Fighting Squadron Eighty-five, May 15, 1944–September 25, 1945* (cover). Anon. N.p., [1946?]. 43 pp., green softcover with black printing and photo of carrier group at sea in background, 35.9 x 27 cm, photos, ports., roster, chronology of events. NDL.

Bombing-Fighting Squadron (VBF) 87

386 *"Another Light Please": History of Bombing-Fighting Squadron 87.* Private collection list. No known copy location.

Torpedo Squadron (VT) 88

387 *Martha's Vineyard to Tokyo: A Historical Record of VT 88.* Cover: Martha's Vineyard to Tokyo, VT 88. Edwin J. Benson, ed. New York: New Era Lithography Co., [1946?] 63 pp., blue, gray, and black softcover with white printing and Avenger flying over ships, spiral binding, 28 x 21.5 cm, photos, ports., map, roster. Private collection.

Fighting Squadron (VF) 89

388 *Pied Pipers: Scrapbook of Fighting Squadron Eighty-nine.* Anon. N.p., [1946?]. 40 leaves, photos. Dabney Catalogue, December 1991: 380. No known copy location.

Composite Squadron (VC) 99

389 *The Seven-League Boots of VC–99.* Cover: Composite Squadron Ninety-nine. Anon. Portland, Oreg.: N.p., 1946. 54 leaves, blue hardcover with gold printing and logo, 28 x 21.7 cm, photos, ports., map. Private collection.

Patrol Bombing Squadron (VPB) 104

390 *Buccaneers of Bombing Squadron 104: The Story of Its First Tour, 10 April 1943–15 April 1944.* Anon. Wichita: McCormick-Armstrong Co., 1944. 38 leaves, 28 cm, photos, ports. Dornbusch 1950: 1061. No known copy location.

391 *The Second Tour of Patrol Bombing Squadron 104, 1 June 1944–1 June 1945* (cover). Anon. N.p., [1945?]. 26 leaves, cover shows a four-engine plane flying over a map of the Pacific Ocean with title in black, 26.5 x 19.5 cm, photos, ports., roster. Dornbusch 1950: 1062. PNAM (photocopy).

392 *Short History of Patrol Bombing Squadron 104 on Its Third Tour, June 1945–October 1945.* Anon. Baltimore: Schneidereith, [1945?]. 24 leaves. Controvich 1992. No known copy location.

Bombing Squadron (VB) 106

393 *Navy Bombing Squadron One Hundred Six VB–106, 1 June 1943–1 June 1944* (cover). Emanuele J. Pasanisi, ed. N.p., [1985?]. 36 leaves, blue hardcover with gold title and wings, 29 x 22.3 cm, photos, ports., map, roster. NDL, PNAM. This is not a true cruise book although it is done in the format of one. It was produced more than forty years after the events.

Patrol Bombing Squadron (VPB) 106

394 *Privateer in the Coconut Navy*. Cover: Patrol Bombing Squadron One Hundred Six. Robert Pusey Hastings. N.p., 1946. 105 pp., 28.6 x 22.2 cm, photos, ports., map, roster. Dornbusch 1951 supp.: 1503. PNAM.

Bombing Squadron (VB) 109

395 *A Pictorial Record of the Combat Duty of Bombing Squadron One Hundred Nine in the Central Pacific, 28 December 1943–14 August 1944, Dedicated to the Officers and Men of the Squadron*. Theodore M. Steele. N.p., [1944?]. 23 x 31 cm, photos, ports. Dornbusch 1950: 1063. No known copy location.

Patrol Bombing Squadron (VPB) 109

396 *A Pictorial Record of the Combat Duty of Patrol Bombing Squadron One Hundred Nine in the Western Pacific, 20 April 1945–15 August 1945, Dedicated to the Officers and Men Who Gave Their Lives That We May Live in Peace*. Cover: Patrol Bombing Squadron 109. Lt. Theodore M. Steele, USNR. New York: General Offset Co., 1946. 32 leaves, flexible blue cover with gold and silver printing, 23 x 30.4 cm, photos, ports., map, roster. Dornbusch 1950: 1064. PNAM.

Patrol Bombing Squadron (VPB) 116

397 *The United States Navy Patrol Bombing Squadron VPB–116: The Blue Raiders*. Clayton J. Whisman. N.p., 1979. 226 pp., loose-leaf binder, 28 x 21.6 cm, photos, accounts of operations. PNAM. This is not a true cruise book, but an account of squadron operations written many years after the events.

Patrol Bombing Squadron (VPB) 117

398 *The Blue Raiders VPB 117, 1944–1945, United States Navy* (cover). Graham B. Squires, ed. N.p., [1985?]. 330 leaves, blue paper cover with black printing and a PB4Y 1, spiral binding, 28 x 21.6 cm, photos, ports., map, roster. PNAM. This is not a true cruise book, but an account written many years after the events.

Patrol Bombing Squadron (VPB) 119

399 *Patrol Bombing Squadron One Hundred Nineteen, 1944–1945*. N.p., [1945?]. 32 leaves, photos, ports. Dabney Catalogue 376, August 1991. No known copy location.

Patrol Bombing Squadron (VPB) 121

400 *Battle Diary of Patrol Bombing Squadron One Hundred Twenty-one, 5 September 1944 to 5 September 1945*. O. M. Corwin, ed. San Diego: Frye & Smith, [1945?]. 55 leaves, 29 cm, photos, ports. Dornbusch 1950: 1064A. No known copy location.

Patrol Bombing Squadron (VPB) 124

401 *Patrol Bombing Squadron One Twenty-four*. N.p., [1945?]. 115 pp., photos, ports., map, roster. Dabney Catalogue, August 1991: 376. No known copy location.

Bombing Squadron (VB) 148

402 *Bombing Squadron 148: Photo Album, August 1943–November 1944*. Private collection list. No known copy location.

Patrol Bombing Squadron (VPB) 153

403 Controvich 1992. No known copy location.

Bombing Squadron (VB) 184

404 *The Second Tour of Bombing Squadron 184, 1 June 1944–1 June 1945*. Private collection list. No known copy location.

Patrol Bombing Squadron (VPB) 210

405 *Patrol Bombing Squadron 210*. This citation was taken from NDL card file although copy could not be located at NDL. No other known reference.

Naval Air Bases and Commands

Aviation Repair and Overhaul Unit 1

406 *Two Degrees From the Middle: The History of Aviation Repair and Overhaul Unit Number One in World War II.* Cover: Two Degrees From the Middle. Anon. St. Paul: Bronson West Advertising, [1946?]. 58 leaves, blue hardcover with gold printing, 28.4 x 21.9 cm, photos, ports., map, roster. PNAM.

Aviation Repair Unit 145

407 *A Lens-Eye View of A.R.U. Navy 145 (Aviation Repair Unit 145).* Private collection list. No known copy location.

Carrier Aircraft Service Unit 16

408 *On the Beam: The Story of One Carrier Aircraft Service Unit.* Cover: On the Beam With CASU Sixteen. Anon. N.p., [1946?]. 52 pp., gray softcover with black printing and logo, 28.4 x 22.9 cm, photos, ports., map, roster. NDL.

Carrier Aircraft Service Unit 54

409 *A History of CASU 54.* Anon. N.p., [1946?]. 14 leaves, white paper cover with brown printing, 15 x 23 cm, presented in brown leather folder (20.6 x 27.3) with gold printing, photos, ports. Dornbusch 1950: 1057. NDL.

Escort Carrier Force, U.S. Pacific Fleet

410 *The Escort Carriers in Action: The Story—in Pictures—of the Escort Carrier Force, U.S. Pacific Fleet, 1945.* Comdr. Price Gilbert, Jr., USNR, ed. Atlanta: Ruralist Press, 1945. 183 pp., blue hardcover with gold printing, 31.1 x 23.3 cm, photos, ports. Dornbusch 1951 supp.: 1488. NDL, PNAM, USNA. See USS *Makin Island* for another edition of this book having a supplement on the flagship.

Naval Air Base, Majuro

411 *Majuro Naval Air Base: An Informal Record of Life on Majuro in Words and Pictures, 1944–1945.* Joseph T. Betlack, ed. N.p., 1945. 39 leaves, 29.9 x 22.5 cm, photos, ports. Smith: 9219. NDL (rebound).

Naval Air Combat Intelligence School, Quonset, Rhode Island

412 *The Life and Times of the Air Combat Intelligence School.* C. W. Mendell. New Haven: Yale University Press, 1946. 121 pp., dust jacket, blue hardcover with blue printing on white background, 23.5 x 15.9 cm, ports., roster. Private collection.

Naval Air Facility, Columbus, Ohio

413 *Naval Air Facility, Columbus, Ohio.* Baton Rouge: Army & Navy Publishing Co., n.d. Army & Navy Publishing Co. List. No known copy location.

Naval Air Facility, Trenton, New Jersey

414 *Test Flight, Mercer Field, Trenton, New Jersey* (cover). Anon. Baton Rouge: Army & Navy Publishing Co., [1945?]. 54 pp., embossed blue hardcover with gold printing and wing emblem, 30.8 x 23.3 cm, photos, ports., roster. NDL.

Naval Air Station, Alameda, California

415 *U.S. Naval Air Station, Alameda, California* (cover). Anon. Baton Rouge: Army & Navy Publishing Co., [1945?]. 146 pp., embossed blue hardcover with gold printing and wings, 30.9 x 23.3 cm, photos, ports. NDL.

Naval Air Station, Anacostia, D.C.

416 *Naval Air Station, Anacostia, D.C.* Baton Rouge: Army & Navy Publishing Co., n.d. Army & Navy Publishing Co. List. No known copy location.

Naval Air Station, Bunker Hill, Indiana

417 *Pinfeather Anniversary Number, U.S. Naval Air Station, Bunker Hill, Indiana* (cover). R. W. Ward, ed. N.p., July 1, 1943. 46 pp., heavy multicolor paper cover with service people saluting in front of control tower, 28.1 x 22 cm, photos, ports. PNAM.

Naval Air Station, Corpus Christi, Texas

418 *The Year Book: U.S. Naval Air Station, Corpus Christi, Texas, 1940–1941* (cover). Anon. Texas Auxiliary of the Navy Relief Society, publisher. N.p., 1941. 102 pp., multicolor paper cover with white printing and view of administrative building, 30.3 x 22.8 cm, photos, ports. NDL, PNAM.

Naval Air Station, Floyd Bennett Field, Brooklyn, New York

419 *Sky Anchors Aweigh*. Cover: The NAS Beam: U.S. Naval Air Station, Floyd Bennett Field, Brooklyn, New York. Public relations staff. Baton Rouge: Army & Navy Publishing Co., [1945?]. 129 pp., dark blue hardcover with gold printing and decoration, 30.8 x 23.2 cm, photos, ports. Private collection.

Naval Air Station, Kaneohe Bay, Oahu T. H.

420 *U.S. Naval Air Station, Kaneohe Bay, Oahu T. H.: Home for Fleet Air Wing Two, WW2*. Private collection list. No known copy location.

Naval Air Station, Livermore, California

421 *Naval Air Station, Livermore, California*. Baton Rouge: Army & Navy Publishing Co., n.d. Army & Navy Publishing Co. List. No known copy location.

Naval Air Station, Norfolk, Virginia

422 *U.S. Naval Air Station, Norfolk, Virginia* (cover). Anon. Baton Rouge: Army & Navy Publishing Co., [1945?]. 220 pp., embossed blue hardcover with gold printing, wings, and embossed airplanes, 30.8 x 23.6 cm, photos, ports., roster. NDL.

Naval Air Station, Norman, Oklahoma

423 *The Smooth Log, Naval Air Station, Norman, Oklahoma* (cover). Anon. Baton Rouge: Army & Navy Publishing Co., [1945?]. 178 pp., blue hardcover with gold printing and wings, 30.9 x 23.3 cm, photos, ports., roster. NDL, PNAM.

Naval Air Station, Quonset Point, Rhode Island

424 *The Story of Quonset*. Cover: U.S. Naval Air Station, Quonset Point, R.I. Anon. Philadelphia: Campus Publishing Co. and Merin-Baliban Studios, [1945?]. 16 leaves, multicolor paper cover with four planes flying over control tower, 26.6 x 19.6 cm, photos. PNAM.

Naval Air Station, San Diego, California

425 *U.S. Naval Air Station, San Diego, California* (cover). Anon. Baton Rouge: Army & Navy Publishing Co., [1946?]. 213 pp., embossed blue hardcover with gold printing and decoration, 30.8 x 23.4 cm, photos, ports., roster. Private collection.

Naval Air Station, Squantum, Massachusetts

426 *The U.S. Naval Air Station Squantum, Squantum, Massachusetts, 1923–1944* (cover). Anon. Baton Rouge: Army & Navy Publishing Co., [1945?]. 63 pp., blue hardcover with gold printing and decoration, 30.8 x 23.3 cm, photos, ports., roster. Private collection.

Naval Air Technical Training Center, Memphis, Tennessee

427 *A Visit to the Naval Air Technical Training Center.* Cover: Naval Air Technical Training Center (NATTC), Memphis: We Keep 'em Flying. Anon. N.p., [1944?]. 24 leaves, blue softcover with dark blue printing and gold decoration, 21 x 27.9 cm, photos, ports. Private collection.

Naval Air Technical Training Center, Norman, Oklahoma

428 *We Keep 'Em Flying: Naval Air Technical Training Center, Norman, Oklahoma* (cover). Anon. Oklahoma City: Travel-Taylor Litho, [1943?]. 16 leaves, gray softcover with black printing and view of planes flying over airport, 21.8 x 28.3 cm, photos, ports. PNAM.

429 *All Hands*, published at Naval Air Technical Training Center, Norman, Oklahoma, 1945. 150 pp., photos. No known copy location. Paul Gaudette Book List 90–167, December 1990.

430 *Naval Air Technical Training Center, Norman, Oklahoma*. Baton Rouge: Army & Navy Publishing Co., n.d. Army & Navy Publishing Co. List. No known copy location.

Naval Air Technical Training Command

431 *Technicians' War: A Picture Story of Naval Air Technical Training Command* (cover). Anon. Atlanta: Albert Love, [1945?]. 48 leaves, blue softcover with white printing and view of plane being loaded with bomb on a carrier deck, 30 x 22.8 cm, photos. No known copy location.

Naval Air Training Center, Pensacola, Florida

432 *Story of the Naval Air Training Center, Pensacola, Florida: "The Annapolis of the Air."* Anon. Ship's Service Department, publisher. N.p., February 1944. 44 pp., paper cover with photo and black printing, 22.5 x 15.3 cm, photos, ports. PNAM.

Naval Air Transport Service

433 *Wings West: Naval Air Transport Service, Book of Original Photographs Prepared for J. W. Reeves, Jr., Rear Admiral, USN*. Anon. N.p., [1946?]. 35 leaves, flexible cover with black and white printing over photo of plane and clouds, spiral binding, 30 x 22.5 cm, photos, ports. PNAM. This is not a true cruise book, but a souvenir book prepared (probably only one) for Rear Admiral Reeves.

434 *Operation Lifeline: History and Development of the Naval Air Transport Service* (title page for both editions). Cover of regular edition: Operation Lifeline: Naval Air Transport Service. Cover of limited edition: Naval Air Transport Service. James Lee. Photos by Joe Rosenthal and U.S. Navy. Chicago and New York: Ziff Davis Publishing Co., 1947. 171 pp., dust jacket, blue hardcover with gold printing, 31.1 x 23.3 cm, photos, ports., map. Dornbusch 1951 supp.: 1505. NDL, PNAM. In addition to the regular edition, 1,000 copies of a limited edition were issued and autographed by several naval dignitaries, including Secretary of the Navy James Forrestal and Admiral Chester W. Nimitz. The PNAM copy is from the limited edition.

Naval Air Cadet Training

For Preflight Training, see Naval Officer Training Section.

Naval Air Cadet Training Program, Corpus Christi, Texas

435 *Mark I of the Slipstream, 1941*. Cover: The Slipstream. J. W. Logan and D. R. Coe, eds. The Aviation Cadets, USNAS Corpus Christi, publisher. N.p., 1942. 190 pp. plus advertising section, blue and cream hardcover with blue printing, 31.2 x 23.5 cm, photos, ports., roster. NDL, PNAM. This is the first edition of the *Slipstream*.

436 *The Slipstream Mark II*. Cover: The Slipstream. J. A. Smith, R. W. Alexander, and J. R. Morris, eds. Aviation Cadet Regiment, USNAS, Corpus Christi, publisher. N.p., 1942. 256 pp. plus advertising section, cream and blue hardcover with blue printing and logo, 31.2 x 23.8 cm, photos, ports., roster. PNAM.

437 *The Mark III Slipstream*. Cover: The Slipstream. D. R. Simmons, R. D. Royal, and L. Townsend, eds. Aviation Cadet Regiment, U.S. Naval Air Training Center, Corpus Christi, Tex., publisher. N.p., [1943?]. 314 pp. plus advertising section, cream and blue hardcover with blue printing and logo, 31.3 x 23.4 cm, photos, ports., roster. NDL, PNAM.

438 *The Slipstream Mark IV Edition.* Cover: The Slipstream. Cy Altman, ed. Aviation Cadet Regiment, U.S. Naval Air Training Center, Corpus Christi, publisher. N.p., [1944?]. 334 pp. plus advertising section, cream and blue hardcover with blue printing and logo, 31.2 x 23.6 cm, photos, ports., roster. NDL, PNAM.

439 *The Slipstream Mark V Edition Presents U.S. Naval Aviation at War.* Cover: The Slipstream. L. A. Merritt, Jr., S. A. Lindsey, and D. N. Sharp, Jr., eds. Cadet Regiment, U.S. Naval Air Training Center, Corpus Christi, publisher. Montgomery, Ala.: Paragon Press [1945?]. 359 pp., cream and blue hardcover with blue printing and logo, 31.3 x 23.8 cm, photos, ports., roster. NDL, PNAM. This is the latest edition in PNAM.

Naval Air Cadet Training Program, Pensacola, Florida

440 *The Flight Jacket, 1940 Yearbook.* Cover (on spine): The Flight Jacket, 1940. William M. Wood, ed. Aviation Cadet Battalion, U.S. Naval Air Station, Pensacola, publisher. N.p., 1940. 94 leaves, embossed white and brown hardcover, 31.3 x 23.6 cm, photos, ports., roster. PNAM.

441 *The Aviation Cadet Regiments of the U.S. Naval Air Stations at Pensacola and Jacksonville, Fla. Present Volume VI of the Flight Jacket, 1941.* Cover (on spine): The Flight Jacket, 1941. Anon. Aviation Cadet Battalion, U.S. Naval Air Stations at Pensacola and Jacksonville, publisher. N.p., 1941. 142 leaves, brown and blue hardcover with logo, 31.4 x 23.5 cm, photos, ports., roster. PNAM.

442 *The Flight Jacket, 1942.* Cover: Flight Jacket for 1942. Anon. Birmingham: Alabama Engraving Co., 1942. 185 pp., embossed blue hardcover with red printing, 31.4 x 23.7 cm, photos, ports., roster. NDL.

443 *The 1943 Flight Jacket, Mark I Edition, USN Air Training Center, Pensacola, Florida.* Cover: Flight Jacket, 1943, Mark I. A. A. Carlson, ed. Air Cadet Battalion NAS, Pensacola, Fla., publisher. N.p., 1943. 186 pp. plus advertising section, tan hardcover with blue, white, and brown printing, 31.4 x 23.7 cm, photos, ports., roster. PNAM.

444 *The 1943 Flight Jacket, Mark II Edition, USN Air Training Center, Pensacola, Florida.* Cover: Flight Jacket, 1943, Mark II. A. A. Carlson, ed. Air Cadet Battalion NAS, Pensacola, publisher. N.p., 1943. 227 pp. plus advertising section, cream and brown hardcover with blue printing, 31.3 x 23.8 cm, photos, ports., roster. PNAM. The *Flight Jacket* of the Pensacola Naval Air Cadets was discontinued for the duration of WW II after the 1943 Mark II edition.

3

Naval Construction Battalion Books

Naval Construction Brigade

Brigades are numbered 1 through 12.

Number 6

445 *Brigade 6 Task on Tinian.* Cover: Sixth Brigade. H. J. Mertens. Commodore P. J. Haloran, publisher. N.p., [1945?]. 22 leaves, tan paper cover with brown printing, 20.2 x 25.9 cm, photos, ports., officer roster. SMPH.

Naval Construction Regiment

Regiments are numbered 1 through 54.

Number 8

446 *The Log 1943–1945, Eighth United States Naval Construction Regiment.* Cover: 1943–1945. Anon. Fort Worth: Southwestern Engraving Co., 1945. 23 leaves, blue hardcover with gold printing and stripe, 31.3 x 23.5 cm, photos, ports., roster. Dornbusch 1950: 1070, Smith: 9931. NDL, SMPH.

Naval Construction Battalions

Battalions are numbered 1 through 148 and 301 through 302.

Number 1

447 *Victory Year Book, 1945.* Anon. Appleton, Wis.: Petersen Press, 1946. 66 pp., 31 cm, photos. Dornbusch 1951 supp.: 1527. No known copy location.

Number 4

448 *Fourth Naval Construction Battalion, United States, June 1942–June 1943* (cover). Anon. N.p., 1943. 12 leaves, yellow paper cover, 15.8 x 21.9 cm, photos, ports., roster. Dabney Catalogue 375, June 1991: 684. SMPH.

449 *Lil' Short Runner Presents the Fourth U.S. Naval Construction Battalion Penguin, 1944–45.* Cover: The Penguin. Anon. Baton Rouge: Army & Navy Pictorial Publishers, [1946?]. 171 pp., yellow-orange hardcover with black printing and logo, 30.9 x 23.5 cm, photos, ports., roster. Dornbusch 1950: 1071, Smith: 9927, Zeigler: 1417. NYPL, SMPH.

Number 5

450 *Journal of Two Journeys* (cover). Anon. Baton Rouge: Army & Navy Pictorial Publishers, 1946. [F. Bode, ed.]. 303 pp., beige hardcover with blue printing, a globe and a palm tree with signs pointing to places where the unit was stationed, 31 x 23.7 cm, photos, ports., map, roster. Dornbusch 1950: 1072, Smith: 9929. SMPH.

Number 6

451 *Saga of the Sixth: A History of the Sixth U.S. Naval Construction Battalion, 1942–1945*. Cover: Saga of the Sixth. J. Paul Blundon, ed. N.p., [1945?]. 97 pp., blue hardcover with gold printing, 26 x 22 cm, photos, ports., map, roster. Ziegler: 1418. NDL, NSP, SMPH.

Number 7

452 *The Men From Coney Island*. Cover: United States Naval 7 Construction Battalion: Company C. James Joseph Langan, ed. Edward Joseph McNamara, publisher. N.p., [1945?]. 16 leaves, gray paper cover, 21.4 x 28.2 cm, photos, ports., roster. SMPH.

453 *Seabees Seventh U.S. Naval Construction Battalion* (cover). Anon. Baton Rouge: Army & Navy Publishing Co., [1946?]. 60 pp., blue hardcover with gold printing and multicolor Seabee logo, 30.8 x 23.1 cm, photos, ports., roster. SMPH, TIL.

454 *The 7th Log: A Battalion Picture Biography*. Cover: 7th Seabees. Ens. James H. Redditt, ed. 7th USN Construction Battalion, 1944–45 operations, publisher. N.p., [1946?]. 66 leaves, blue hardcover, 29.2 x 22.2 cm, photos, roster. SMPH, TIL.

Number 8

455 *Eighth Naval Construction Battalion: Battling Builders, 1942–1943* (cover). Anon. N.p., [1943?]. 12 leaves, white paper cover with black printing, 21.2 x 27.9 cm, ports., roster. SMPH.

456 *Pieces of Eight, 1942–1945*. Cover: Pieces of Eight: Pictorial Review of the Eighth U.S. Naval Construction Battalion. Comdr. William T. Powers, CEC, USNR, publisher. A. W. Gallo, ChC, adviser. Allentown, Pa.: Schlechter's, [1946?]. 60 leaves, embossed maroon hardcover with gold printing, 31.1 x 23.4 cm, photos, ports., map, roster. Dornbusch 1950: 1073, Smith: 9932, Zeigler: 1420. NYPL, SMPH.

457 *The Log, 1943–1945*. Anon. N.p., [1945?]. 46 pp. Controvich 1992. No known copy location.

Number 11

458 *Southern Cross Duty: Eleventh USN Construction Battalion, 1942–1944*. Anon. Eleventh U.S. Naval Construction Battalion, publisher. Baton Rouge: Army & Navy Pictorial Publishers, [1946?]. 103 pp., brown and blue hardcover with brown and blue printing, 31 x 23.4 cm, photos, ports., map, roster. Dornbusch 1950: 1074, Smith: 9936. NDL, SMPH.

Number 13

459 *U.S. Naval Construction Battalion 13, July 13, 1942* (cover). Anon. N.p., 1942, 16 leaves, paper cover with multicolor map of Alaska and Aleutians, 16.5 x 22.5 cm, photos, ports., roster. Dornbusch 1951 supp.: 1512, Smith: 9937. SMPH.

460 *Pictorial Record of the 13th Naval Construction Battalion, 1942–1943*. Anon. N.p., [1943?]. 18 leaves, Controvich 1992. No known copy location. The author has not seen this book so further details are lacking. It is possible that this reference is the same as the one above, but this seems unlikely.

461 *13th USNCB Second Cruise*. G. W. Riedell, ed. San Francisco: Schwabacher-Frey Co., 1946. 200 pp., blue hardcover with gold printing, 23.7 x 31.1 cm, photos, ports., map, roster. Dornbusch 1950: 1075, Smith: 9938. NYPL (rebound), SMPH.

Number 15

462 *All This and Twenty Per Cent: The Pictorial Story of the Fifteenth United States Naval Construction Battalion in the Southwest Pacific*. Anon. Baton Rouge: Army & Navy Publishing Co., [1945?]. 167 pp., black hardcover with multicolored logo, 31 x 23 cm, photos, ports. Dornbusch 1950: 1076, Smith: 9939. SMPH.

463 *Just A Stone's Throw From Tokyo: A Pictorial Story of the 15th U.S. Naval Construction Battalion's Second Tour of Duty in the Pacific*. Cover: 15 CB. Compiled and edited by Howard A. Friedman. Art by Berger S. Fagenstrom. Photography by Howard A. Friedman and Merritt D. Hadley. Baton Rouge: Army & Navy Pictorial Publishers, 1946. 134 pp., cream hardcover with red printing and multicolor logo, 30.8 x 23.3 cm, photos, ports., map, roster. Dornbusch 1950: 1077, Smith: 9940. NYPL, SMPH.

Number 16

464 *16th U.S. Naval Construction Battalion.* Cover: 16th Construction Battalion Yearbook. Anon. N.p., [1945?]. 84 leaves, blue softcover with silver printing, 26.9 x 19.5 cm, photos, ports., roster. Dornbusch 1950: 1078, Smith: 9941. SMPH.

Number 18

465 *The Odyssey: Eighteenth U.S. Naval Construction Battalion* (cover). G. F. Nichols, ed. San Francisco: Schwabacher-Frey Co., 1946. 94 pp., brown hardcover with gold printing and Maori art decoration, 23.5 x 30.8 cm, photos, ports., map. Dornbusch 1950: 1079, Smith: 9943, Zeigler: 1421. SMPH, TIL.

Number 20

466 *Log of the 20th U.S. Naval Construction Battalion First Cruise, 1942–1944.* Cover: 20th Battalion 1st Cruise, 1942–1944. CBM James F. McLoughlin. Baton Rouge: Army & Navy Publishing Co., [1945?]. 99 pp., embossed blue hardcover with multicolor Seabee logo, 30.8 x 23.5 cm, photos, ports., map, roster. Dornbusch 1951 supp.: 1512-A. NDL, NYPL.

467 [20th Battalion 2nd Cruise]. Baton Rouge: Army & Navy Publishing Co. Army & Navy Publishing Co. List. No known copy location.

Number 21

468 *21st U.S. Naval Construction Battalion, Souvenir Annual, 1942–1943* (cover). PhoM1c E. D. Nease, ed. N.p., [1944?]. 18 leaves, blue paper cover with dark blue printing and logo, 18.4 x 28 cm, photos, ports., roster. Dornbusch 1950: 1080, Smith: 9946. NYPL, SMPH.

469 *The Blackjack, 1944–1945: A Story About and Published by the 21st U.S. Naval Construction Battalion.* Cover: The Blackjack, 1944–1945. Y3c G. H. Porter, ed. Baton Rouge: Army & Navy Pictorial Publishers, [1946?]. 190 pp., gray hardcover with black and red printing, 30.8 x 23.5 cm, photos, ports., map, roster. Dornbusch 1950: 1081, Smith: 9947, Zeigler: 1422. NDL, SMPH.

Number 22

470 *Sitkattu: An Account of the Activities of the Twenty-second U.S. Naval Construction Battalion From Its Inception to the Completion of Its First Tour of Duty Overseas, 1942–1943–1944.* Cover: Sitkattu. Anon. San Francisco: Schwabacher-Frey Co., [1945?]. 40 leaves, blue softcover with white printing and map of Aleutians and Japan in background, 28.5 x 22.1 cm, photos, ports., roster. Dornbusch 1950: 1082, Smith: 9948. SMPH.

Number 23

471 *23rd Battalion 1944* (cover). John A. Alexander, ed. N.p., 1944. 47 pp., blue and gold hardcover with blue printing and gold map of Alaska and Aleutian Islands in the background, 24.1 x 31.5 cm, photos, ports., roster. SMPH.

472 *23rd USNCB.* Lt. (jg) Albert Wilson, Jr., ed. N.p., [1944?]. 162 pp., brown hardcover with red, white, and blue shield logo, 23.8 x 31.5 cm, photos, ports., map, roster. Dornbusch 1950: 1083, Smith: 9949. NYPL (film) and SMPH.

Number 24

473 *The Twenty-fourth United States Naval Construction Battalion.* Cover: The Twenty-fourth U.S. Naval Construction Battalion, 1942–1945. Anon. Baton Rouge: Army & Navy Pictorial Publishers, 1946. 244 pp., blue hardcover with embossed title, flag and shield, 30.9 x 23.6 cm, photos, ports., map, roster. Dornbusch 1951 supp.: 1513, Smith: 9950, Zeigler: 1423. SMPH, USNA (rebound).

Number 25

474 *25 CB Pacific Diary* (cover). Eric De Reynier, ed. N.p., [1945?]. 125 pp., blue hardcover with gold printing and shield, 31.1 x 23.5 cm, photos, ports., map, roster. Dornbusch 1950: 1084, Smith: 9951, Zeigler: 1424. SMPH.

Number 26

475 *Service Record of the 26th Naval Construction Battalion, 1942–1943.* Cover: Twenty-sixth Construction Battalion. Lt. (jg) R. E. Walters, CEC, USNR, ed. N.p., [1944?]. 34 leaves, cream hardcover with blue printing and man with sledge standing on Guadalcanal Island, 20.9 x 27.1 cm, photos, ports., map, roster. Dornbusch 1950: 1085, Smith: 9952. SMPH, USNA (rebound).

Number 27

476 *Danger, Fighting Men at Work: A Work-a-Day Tale of How the Job Was Actually Done by the 27th Seabees as Told by Willard G. Triest to Commander Edward J. Doherty*. Cover: 27th NCB: Danger, Fighting Men At Work. Willard G. Triest. Baton Rouge: Army & Navy Pictorial Publishers, [1946?]. 196 pp., black hardcover printed in yellow, red, and white, 30.8 x 23.5 cm, photos, ports., map, roster. Dornbusch 1950: 1086, Smith: 9953. NDL, SMPH.

477 *Ready on the Right: A True Story of a Naturalist-Seabee on the Islands of Kodiak, Unalaska, Adak, Tanaga, Oahu, Eniwetok, Guam, Mogmog (Ulithi), and Okinawa*. Ralph J. Donahue. Kansas City, Mo.: Smith Printing Co., [1946?]. 194 pp., 21 cm, photos, map, Dornbusch 1951 supp.: 1514. No known copy location.

Number 28

478 [Combat History of the 28th NCB]. Baton Rouge: Army & Navy Publishing Co., [1945?]. Army & Navy Publishing Co. List. No known copy location.

Number 29

479 *Presenting in Pictures the Activities of the Twenty-ninth United States Naval Construction Battalion Base Builders, 1942–1944*. Cover: 29th United States Naval Construction Battalion, 1942–1944. Anon. N.p., [1945?]. 20 leaves, plastic cover, red, brown, and heavy, black inner paper cover, spiral binding, 27.2 x 21.1 cm, photos, ports., roster. Dornbusch 1950: 1087. Smith: 9955. NDL, SMPH.

Number 30

480 *The 30th Log: A Battalion Biography*. Cover: The 30th Log. Spine: The 30th Log, June 1944. Lt. A. J. P. Martini, CEC, USNR, ed. New York: Robert W. Kelly Publishing Corp., 1944. 283 pp., blue hardcover with gold printing, 27.3 x 20.1 cm, photos, ports., map, roster. NDL, SMPH.

481 *The 30th Log: A Battalion Biography, Volume Two*. Cover: The 30th Log. Spine: The 30th Log, 1944–1945. Lt. A. J. P. Martini, CEC, USNR, ed. Issued by the 30th USN Construction Battalion. New York: Robert W. Kelly Publishing Corp., 1945. 375 pp., blue hardcover with gold printing, 27.2 x 20.2 cm, photos, ports., map, roster. Dornbusch 1950: 1088, Smith: 9956. NDL, SMPH.

Number 31

482 *The 31st Spearhead Naval Construction Battalion.* Anon. New York: Comet Press, [1946?]. 87 leaves, maroon hardcover with gold-embossed printing, 31.2 x 22.9 cm, photos, ports., map, roster. Dornbusch 1950: 1089, Smith: 9958. NYPL, SMPH.

Number 32

483 *Thirty-second Construction Battalion, United States Navy.* Cover: 32nd U.S. Naval Construction Battalion. Anon. N.p., [1945?]. 70 leaves, blue softcover with white printing and map of Aleutian Islands in background, 21.3 x 25.9 cm, photos, ports., roster. SMPH.

Number 33

484 *The Log of the Thirty-third U.S. Naval Construction Battalion.* Cover: The Log of the 33rd United States Construction Battalion. W. K. Wilson, ed. N.p., [1945?]. 40 pp., tan softcover with black printing and palm tree and Seabee logo, 27.9 x 21.4 cm, photos, ports., map, roster. Dornbusch 1950: 1090, Smith: 9961. NYPL, SMPH.

485 *33rd U.S. Naval Construction Battalion: The Log.* Cover: 33rd Seabees. Lt. W. K. Wilson, CEC, ed. Baton Rouge: Army & Navy Pictorial Publishers, [1945?]. 85 pp., embossed blue hardcover with multicolor Seabee logo, 30.9 x 23.3 cm, photos, ports., map, roster. Dornbusch 1950: 1091, Smith: 9960. NYPL, SMPH.

Number 34

486 *Thirty-fourth U.S. Naval Construction Battalion.* CCM Frasia Davis Trice, and CY Thurlow Benjamin Simons, eds. Comdr. Lester M. Marx, publisher. San Francisco: Schwabacher-Frey Co., 1946. 42 leaves, blue hardcover with title printed in gold, 30.9 x 23.5 cm, photos, ports., roster. Dornbusch 1950: 1092, Smith: 9962, Zeigler: 1250. SMPH.

Number 35

487 *35th U.S. Naval Construction Battalion* (cover). Anon. Baton Rouge: Army & Navy Publishing Co., [1944?]. 64 pp., blue hardcover with gold printing and embossed Seabee logo, 30.8 x 23.3 cm, photos, ports., roster. Dornbusch 1950: 1093, Smith: 9964. NDL, SMPH.

488 *Pictorial Review.* Anon. N.p., [1945?]. Controvich 1992. No known copy location.

Number 36

489 *36th Naval Construction Battalion, January, 1945* (cover). Anon. Baton Rouge: Army & Navy Publishing Co., [1945?]. 56 pp., embossed blue hardcover with gold printing and multicolor Seabee logo, 30.8 x 23.3 cm, photos, ports., roster. Dornbusch 1951 supp.: 1515, Smith: 9965. NDL, SMPH.

Number 37

490 *37th Seabees* (cover). Anon. Baton Rouge: Army & Navy Publishing Co., [1946?]. 61 pp., embossed blue hardcover with multicolor Seabee logo, 30.9 x 23.3 cm, photos, ports., roster. Dornbusch 1951 supp.: 1516, Smith: 9966. SMPH.

Number 38

491 *The 38th NCB Saga, 38th Naval Construction Battalion as a Permanent Record of Their First Tour of Duty*. Cover: Saga of the 38th CB. R. M. Brooks, Welfare Officer, ed. Officer-in-charge L. A. Cline, publisher. San Francisco: A. Carlisle & Co., [1944?]. 160 pp., embossed blue hardcover with gold printing and logo, 31.2 x 23.5 cm, photos, ports., roster. Dornbusch 1950: 1094, Smith: 9967. NDL, SMPH.

492 *2nd Saga of the 38 NCB: Aleutians: Adak, Kodiak, Kiska, Oahu, Marianas, Tinian; Japan: Sasebo, Kure, Yokohama*. Cover: Saga. William A. Herrmann, ed. N.p., [1945?]. 135 pp., blue hardcover with silver printing, 31 x 23.5 cm, photos, ports., map, roster. Dornbusch 1950: 1095, Smith: 9968. NYPL, SMPH.

Number 40

493 *Souwespac 40th Naval Construction Battalion, Oct. 1942—Sept. 1944, Published by the Fortieth Naval Construction Battalion*. Cover: 40th USNCB SOUWESPAC. Lt. Comdr. Henry J. Rumbarger, officer-in-charge; Lt. George W. Birch, editor in charge of publication. Designed and edited by Maurice Bailey. N.p., [1946?]. 72 leaves, blue hardcover with gold printing, 31 x 23.7 cm, photos, ports., map, roster. Dornbusch 1950: 1097, Smith: 9970. NDL, SMPH.

494 *POA 40th CB 40th Naval Construction Battalion*. Cover: POA 40CB. Designed and edited by Maurice S. Bailey. Photographs by Clifford Baughman and John Hynd. Text and staff work by Richard W. Hoppe. N.p., [1945?]. 56 leaves, black hardcover with gold printing, 31.2 x 23.6 cm, photos, map, roster. Dornbusch 1950: 1096, Smith: 9969. SMPH.

Number 42

495 *42nd Naval Construction Battalion Year Book, 1944–1945.* Cover: The 42nd United States Naval Construction Battalion: Skilled Men Under Arms. Thomas L. Hogan, ed. Milwaukee: Arandell Litho, [1947?]. 155 pp., embossed cream hardcover with black printing and eagle, 30.8 x 23.2 cm, photos, ports., map, roster. Dornbusch 1951 supp.: 1517, Smith: 9972, Zeigler: 1427. NYPL, SMPH.

496 *Forty-second Battalion CB AMADU* (cover). Y1c E. P. Organ, ed. Seattle: Farwest Lithograph & Print Co., [1945?]. 150 pp., embossed blue hardcover with gold printing, 28.5 x 22 cm, photos, ports., map, roster. Dornbusch 1950: 1098, Smith: 9971. NYPL, SMPH.

Number 43

497 *The Log: 43rd Construction Battalion, 1942–1946* (cover). Lt. M. P. Clouse, MC, USNR, ed. Baton Rouge: Army & Navy Pictorial Publishers, [1946?]. 153 pp., brown hardcover with embossed title and emblem printed in green, 30.9 x 23 cm, photos, ports., roster. Dornbusch 1950: 1099, Smith: 9973, Zeigler: 1428. SMPH, USNA.

Number 44

498 *United States Naval 44 Construction Battalion* (cover). Anon. N.p., [1945?]. 165 pp., blue hardcover with gold and red printing, 31.1 x 23.8 cm, photos, ports., map, roster. Dornbusch 1950: 1100, Smith: 9974. SMPH.

Number 45

499 *Chechakho to Sourdough: The Story of the Forty-fifth United States Naval Construction Battalion in Alaska, World War II.* Cover: 45th Battalion Seabees, United States Navy. Lt. (jg) W. H. Mitchell, ed. San Francisco: A. Carlisle & Co., 1944. 188 pp., black hardcover with red, white, and blue decoration, 31.2 x 23.8 cm, photos, ports., map. Dornbusch 1950: 1101, Smith: 9975. SMPH.

Number 46

500 *The Anxiety of the 46th U.S. Naval Construction Battalion, 18 November 1942–1 May 1945.* Cover: The Anxiety. Anon. San Francisco: Hooper Print Co., [1946?]. 132 pp., blue hardcover with gold printing and multicolor logo, 39.8 x 22.3 cm, photos, ports., roster. Dornbusch 1950: 1102, Smith: 9976. NYPL, SMPH.

501 *Following Invasions: Being an Account of the Forty-sixth Seabee Battalion in the Southwest Pacific.* Cover: Following Invasions. Jones G. Emery. Oklahoma City: Harlow Publishing, [1946?]. 215 pp., blue hardcover with gold printing, 20.1 x 14.3 cm, photos. Private collection.

Number 48

502 *Souvenir Edition Tradewinds* (cover). MM3c Jack W. Turner, ed. Comdr. Joshua T. Davis, publisher. N.p., [1945?]. 32 leaves, white softcover with purple printing and multicolor decoration, 28 x 21.5 cm, photos, ports., roster. SMPH. This book was also issued as *Tradewinds, 48th USNCB,* blue hardcover, 28.8 x 21.2 cm.

Number 49

503 *Bermuda Cruise, Published by the 49th U.S. Naval Construction Battalion.* Cover: Bermuda Cruise, 49th Naval Construction Battalion, 1943. Ens. Lester A. Robb, ed. New York: F. Hubner & Co., [1943?]. 94 pp., blue hardcover with gold printing, 31 x 23.4 cm, photos, ports., roster. Dornbusch 1950: 1103, Smith: 9977. NDL, SMPH.

Number 50

504 *50th U.S. Naval Construction Battalion.* Cover: The Fiftieth Seabees. Walter Drysdale, ed. San Francisco: A. Carlisle & Co., [1945?]. 108 pp., blue hardcover with black printing, 23.5 x 31 cm, photos, ports., roster. Dornbusch 1950: 1104, Smith: 9978, Zeigler: 1429. NDL, NSP, NYPL, SMPH, USNA (rebound).

Number 52

505 *52 NCB* (cover). Anon. St. Louis, Mo.: [1945?]. 132 pp., embossed blue hardcover with gold printing, 28.4 x 21.8 cm, photos, ports., map, roster. Dornbusch 1950: 1105, Smith: 9979. NYPL, SMPH. A handwritten note in the NYPL copy states, "Printed by Farwest Lithograph & Printing Co., Seattle, Wash. June '44."

Number 53

506 *History of the 53rd N.C.B., February 1943 to February 1946.* Cover: 53rd U.S. Naval Construction Battalion: The Marine Seabee, 1st MAC. Anon. Baton Rouge: Army & Navy Pictorial Publishers, 1946. 121 pp., embossed blue hardcover with gold printing and multicolor logo, 30.9 x 23.3 cm, photos, ports., roster. Dornbusch 1950: 1106, Smith: 9980. NSP, NYPL, SMPH.

507 *Bikini Atoll Atom Bomb Test, 53rd United States Naval Construction Battalion, Bikini Atoll, 1946* (cover). Comdr. J. D. Burky. N.p., 1946. 9 leaves, white paper cover with black printing and photograph of unit sign, 27.9 x 21.8 cm, photos, ports. NYPL, SMPH. This is an early post-WW II book covering activity at the Bikini atomic bomb test.

Number 54

508 *A Record of the Deeds, Action, and Experiences of the Fifty-fourth United States Naval Construction Battalion in North Africa*. Cover: Fifty-fourth United States Naval Construction Battalion. Ens. H. E. Phillips, ed. New York: Polygraphic Co., [1944?]. 132 pp., blue hardcover with gold printing, 33.5 x 25.7 cm, photos, ports., map, roster. Dornbusch 1950: 1107. NYPL, SMPH.

Number 55

509 *The 55 Seabees, 1942–1945, Published by the Officers and Men of the United States Naval Construction Battalion 55*. Cover: The 55th Seabees, 1942–1945. Y1c Delmas W. Abbott. Baton Rouge: Army & Navy Publishing Co., [1945?]. 169 pp., blue hardcover with gold printing and decoration, 23.5 x 28.5 cm, photos, ports., maps, roster. Dornbusch 1950: 1108, Smith: 9981, Zeigler: 1430. NDL, SMPH.

Number 57

510 *SOPAC Saga, 57th Seabees, 1942–1945*. Cover: SOPAC Saga, 57th CB. Lt. Lawrence J. Bradd, ed. San Francisco: Schwabacher-Frey Co., 1946. 182 pp., blue hardcover with gold tractor and title in blue on gold background, 28.6 x 22.2 cm, photos, ports., roster. Dornbusch 1950: 1109, Smith: 9982, Zeigler: 1431. NDL, SMPH, USNA.

Number 58

511 *History of the Fifty-eighth United States Naval Construction Battalion, 1942–1945*. Cover: 58 USNCB. C. Edward Gideon, ed. Photographs by Miguel Gasco. Brooklyn, N.Y.: Foxcroft Commercial Press, [1950?]. 252 pp., black hardcover with gold printing and Seabee logo, 27.8 x 22.1 cm, photos, maps. Dornbusch 1951 supp.: 1518, Smith: 9983, Zeigler: 1432. SMPH.

Number 60

512 *The 60th Seabees: An Album of Memories*. Cover: 60th Seabees. Anon. New York: Business Photo Reproduction Co., [1945?]. 125 pp., blue hardcover with multicolor Seabee logo, 28.5 x 22 cm, photos, ports., roster. Dornbusch 1950: 1110, Smith: 9984. NYPL, SMPH.

513 *History of the Sixtieth Naval Construction Battalion: 60th Seabees* (cover). Anon. N.p., [1946?]. 43 pp., black fiberboard cover with yellow printing and multicolor logo, 30.3 x 25.5 cm, officer roster. SMPH (2 copies). This book is typewritten sheets with fiberboard covers. It would appear that only a few of these were made.

Number 61

514 *Sixty-first Sea Foam: A Log Book Originated and Compiled by Members of Sixty-first U.S. Naval Construction Battalion*. Cover: 61. Davis R. Webb, ed. Baton Rouge: Army & Navy Pictorial Publishers, [1946?]. 218 pp., blue hardcover with multicolor logo and printing, 30.9 x 23.7 cm, photos, ports., roster. Dornbusch 1950: 1111, Smith: 9985. SMPH.

Number 62

515 *We Did: The Story of the 62nd NCB, December 7, 1942 to September 15, 1945*. Cover: Sixty Seconds: CB Minute-Men. Meredith Trent, CCM, USNR, ed. Baton Rouge: Army & Navy Pictorial Publishers, [1946?]. 191 pp., olive hardcover with red printing and decoration, 30.7 x 23.4 cm, photos, ports., roster. Dornbusch 1950: 1112, Smith: 9986. NYPL.

Number 63

516 *63 United States Naval Construction Battalion: Can Do!* (cover). Lt. Roy A. Burgess, ed. New York: Robert W. Kelly Publishing Corp., [1946?]. 161 pp., blue hardcover with gold printing and decoration, 27.3 x 20.3 cm, photos, ports., map, roster. Dornbusch 1950: 1113, Smith: 10001, Zeigler: 1433. NYPL, SMPH.

Number 64

517 *History of the Battalion, 1942, 1943, 1944, 1945*. Cover: 64th U.S.N.C.B., 1942–1946. Anon. Baton Rouge: Army & Navy Pictorial Publishers, [1946?]. 116 pp., blue hardcover with red, white, and blue printing and dice, 30.9 x 23.3 cm, photos, ports., map, roster. Dornbusch 1950: 1114, Smith: 10002. SMPH.

Number 66

518 *The Sixty-sixth Construction Battalion Yearbook, Published by the 66th Naval Construction Battalion as a Permanent Record of Its First Tour of Duty*. Cover: 66th U.S. Naval Construction Battalion. William L. Ahlert, ed. N.p., [1945?]. 205 pp., white hardcover with gold printing and shield logo, 36.3 x 27.3 cm, photos, ports., roster. Dornbusch 1950: 1115, Smith: 10003. SMPH.

Number 67

519 *Pictorial Log: 67th Naval Construction Battalion*. Cover: 67th United States Naval Construction Battalion. Anon. Baton Rouge: Army & Navy Pictorial Publishers, [1946?]. 101 pp., blue hardcover with gold printing, 31 x 23 cm, photos, ports., map, roster. Dornbusch 1950: 1116, Smith: 10004. SMPH.

Number 68

520 *68 Seabees, U.S. Naval Construction Battalion*. Cover: 68th Seabees. Anon. N.p., [1945?]. 59 pp., blue softcover with gold printing and decoration, 26.5 x 20.8 cm, photos, ports. Dornbusch 1951 supp.: 1519, Smith: 10005. SMPH.

521 *68th U.S. Naval Construction Battalion* (cover). Anon. Baton Rouge: Army & Navy Publishing Co., [1946?]. 61 pp., embossed blue hardcover with gold printing, 30.9 x 23.4 cm, photos, ports., roster. NDL, SMPH.

Number 69

522 *69 U.S. Naval Construction Battalion Victory*. Cover: Cruise Log: 69th U.S. Naval Construction Battalion, European Theatre of Operations. Anon. N.p., [1945?]. 263 pp., blue hardcover with silver printing, 28.7 x 20.7 cm, photos, ports., maps, roster. Dornbusch 1950: 1117, Smith: 10007. NYPL, SMPH.

523 *The 69th U.S. Naval Construction Battalion*. Anon. Baton Rouge: Army & Navy Publishing Co., [1945?]. 61 pp., Smith: 10006. No known copy location.

Number 70

524 *Seabees*. Cover: USN 70th Construction Battalion. Anon. Baton Rouge: Army & Navy Publishing Co., [1944?]. 75 pp., blue hardcover with gold printing, 30.9 x 23.2 cm, photos, ports., roster. Dornbusch 1950: 1521, Smith: 10008. SMPH.

525 *USN 70th Construction Battalion, Pacific Edition, Volume II.* Anon. Baton Rouge: Army & Navy Pictorial Publishers, [1946?]. 83 pp., embossed blue hardcover with gold printing, 30.8 x 23 cm, photos, ports., maps, roster. Dornbusch 1950: 1118, Smith: 10009. NYPL, SMPH.

Number 71

526 *U.S. Navy 71st Battalion.* Robert O. Lunnard and Frank A. Donovan. N.p., [1945?]. 71 leaves, blue hardcover with gold printing and decoration, 31 x 23.2 cm, photos, ports., roster. Dornbusch 1951 supp.: 1522. NYPL, SMPH.

527 *U.S. Navy 71st Construction Battalion.* James R. Schuyler et al., eds. N.p., [1945?]. Controvich 1992. No known copy location.

Number 73

528 *The Story of the Seventy-third United States Naval Construction Battalion: New Caledonia, Guadalcanal, Munda Point, New Georgia Islands, Banika Islands, Russell Islands, Peleliu Islands, Palau Island.* Cover: 73rd Seabees. Anon. Baton Rouge: Army & Navy Pictorial Publishers, [1946?]. 114 pp., tan hardcover with brown printing, 30.9 x 23.4 cm, photos, ports., map, roster. Dornbusch 1950: 1119, Smith: 10010. NDL, NYPL, SMPH.

Number 74

529 *74th Battalion in Review, 1943–1944* (cover). Anon. Berkeley: Lederer Street & Zeus, [1945?]. 158 pp., olive hardcover with gold printing and anchor, 30 x 44 cm, photos, ports., roster. Dornbusch 1950: 1120, Smith: 10011. SCM, SMPH.

Number 75

530 *Pacific Album, 75th Seabees.* John J. Kasap et al., eds. N.p., [1945?]. 196 pp., embossed blue hardcover with silver and green printing and Seabee logo, 28.8 x 22.9 cm, photos, ports., map, roster. Dornbusch 1950: 1121, Smith: 10012. NDL, NSP, SMPH.

Number 76

531 *Seventy-sixth Construction, United States Navy.* Cover: Seventy-sixth Construction Battalion, United States Navy. Chaplain Evaristus B. Olberding, ed. N.p., [1945?]. 62 leaves, blue hardcover with gold printing and decoration, 31.1 x 23.4 cm, photos, ports., roster. Dornbusch 1950: 1122, Smith: 10013. NYPL, SMPH.

Number 77

532 *We Did: The Story of the 77th Naval Construction Battalion*. Cover: We Did: 77th U.S. Navy Construction Battalion. Thomas A. Ceplikas, ed. Baton Rouge: Army & Navy Pictorial Publishing Co., [1946?]. 287 pp., embossed blue hardcover with gold printing and emblem, 31 x 24 cm, photos, ports., roster. Dornbusch 1950: 1123, Smith: 10014. NDL, SMPH.

Number 78

533 *Seventy-eighth Construction Battalion, United States Navy*. Cover: Battalion Log, Seventy-eighth U.S. Naval Construction Battalion. Anon. Boston: Rand Avery-Gordon Taylor, [1945?]. 155 pp., embossed blue hardcover with silver printing and logo, 28.5 x 22.2 cm, photos, ports., map, roster. Dornbusch 1950: 1124, Smith: 10015, NYPL, SMPH.

Number 79

534 *The Seventy-ninth United States Naval Construction Battalion*. Cover: 79th USN Construction Battalion. Lt. (jg) W. R. Kramer, ed. Seattle: Deers Press, [1944?]. 100 pp., blue and white hardcover with title printed on shield logo, 28 x 21.6 cm, photos, ports., map, roster. Dornbusch 1951 supp.: 1523, Smith: 10016. NYPL (film), SMPH.

Number 80

535 *Seabees Log of the Cruise, 80th USN Construction Battalion, 1943–1944* (cover). Chief Carpenter Howard E. Webb, ed. Providence: Blackford Engraving & Electrotype Co., [1944?]. 129 pp., embossed blue hardcover with gold printing and emblem, 31 x 23.5 cm, photos, ports., map, roster. SMPH.

Number 82

536 *Eighty-second U.S. Naval Construction Battalion, 1943–1945*. Harry Heathcock, ed. Greensburg, Pa.: Chas. Henry Printing Co., 1946. 69 leaves, blue hardcover with gold printing, 31.2 x 23.6 cm, photos, ports., roster. Dornbusch 1950: 1125, Smith: 10017, Zeigler: 1434. NYPL, SMPH.

Number 83

537 *83rd Battalion Year Book* (cover). Anon. Port of Spain, Trinidad: Guardian Commercial Printery, [1945?]. 116 pp., green hardcover with photograph of four sailors and flag, 36 x 29 cm, photos, ports., roster. Dornbusch 1950: 1126, Smith: 10018. SMPH.

Number 84

538 *The United States Naval Construction Battalion 84.* Cover: 2nd Anniversary, 1945. Franz A. Werner. Lt. Comdr. Roger F. Neal, publisher. 84th Seabee Print Shop, [1945?]. 28 leaves, green softcover with white printing and candle, 26 x 18.7 cm, photos, ports., roster. Dornbusch 1950: 1127, Smith: 10019. SMPH.

539 *The United States Naval Construction Battalion 84.* Anon. Baton Rouge: Army & Navy Publishing Co., 1946. 78 pp., Controvich 1992. No known copy location.

Number 85

540 *United States Naval Construction Battalion 85* (cover). Anon. Nashville: Benson Printing Co., [1945?]. 80 pp., blue hardcover with the number 85 embossed in gold, 31.8 x 23.1 cm, photos, ports., roster. SMPH.

541 *The Eighty-fifth United States Naval Construction Battalion.* Cover: 85 United States Naval Construction Battalion. Charles Scifres, ed. N.p., [1946?]. 78 pp., black hardcover with the number 85 in gold, 30.9 x 23.5 cm, photos, ports., roster. Dornbusch 1950: 1128, Smith: 10020, Zeigler: 1435. NYPL, SMPH.

Number 86

542 *Battalioneer.* Anon. San Francisco: [1944?]. 88 leaves, 31 cm, photos, ports. Dornbusch 1951 supp.: 1524. No known copy location.

Number 87

543 *The Earthmovers: A Chronicle of the 87th Seabee Battalion in World War II.* Cover: The Earthmovers, 1943–1945, USN Construction Battalion 87. Anon. Baton Rouge: Army & Navy Pictorial Publishers, [1946?]. 368 pp., blue hardcover with gold printing and the number 87 in red, 30.9 x 23.8 cm, photos, ports., map, roster. Dornbusch 1950: 1129, Smith: 10021. SMPH.

Number 88

544 *In Review: A History and Pictorial Account of the 88th Naval Construction Battalion.* Cover: In Review, 88th. Anon. Jacksonville: M. G. Lewis Printing Co., [1945?]. 72 leaves, embossed blue hardcover with red and blue printing and silhouette of ship in background, 31.2 x 27.2 cm, photos, ports., roster. Dornbusch 1950: 1130, Smith: 10022. NYPL, SMPH.

Number 90

545 *90th USN Construction Battalion: Its History and Accomplishments, 1943–1945*. Cover: 90th Seabees, USNCB. Anon. Baton Rouge: Army & Navy Publishing Co., 1946. 96 leaves, brown and blue hardcover with embossed logo and white printing, 30.8 x 23.4 cm, photos, ports. Dornbusch 1950: 1131, Smith: 10023, Zeigler: 1436. SMPH.

Number 91

546 *A History of the Ninety-first Naval Construction Battalion, 1943–1945*. Cover: 91st U.S. Naval Construction Battalion. Anon. New York: Winson Associates, [1946?]. 164 pp., embossed blue hardcover with gold printing, 31.2 x 23.6 cm, photos, ports., roster. Dornbusch 1950: 1132, Smith: 10024, Zeigler: 1437. NDL, SMPH.

Number 92

547 *The Ninety-second Naval Construction Battalion Log for the Year Ending the Twenty-eighth of May, Nineteen Hundred and Forty-four*. Cover: 92 United States Naval Construction Battalion. [K. C. Strebig, ed.]. Anon. N.p., [1945?]. 129 pp., white hardcover with brown printing, loose-leaf binding with screws, 22.5 x 28.8 cm, photos, ports., roster. Dornbusch 1950: 1133, Smith: 10025. NYPL (film), SMPH. This book includes the "Log for the Year Ending Twenty-eighth of May, Nineteen Hundred and Forty-five."

Number 93

548 *Pacific Duty: A Book of Record and Review of the Activities and Achievements of the Ninety-third United States Naval Construction Battalion*. Cover: 93 CB Battalion. G. E. Pappas, ed. Huntington Park, Calif.: Lester C. Nielson Co., 1946. 159 pp., embossed blue hardcover with gold printing and emblem, 31 x 23.2 cm, photos, ports., roster. Dornbusch 1950: 1134, Smith: 10026. NDL, SMPH.

Number 94

549 *Pacific Duty 94th*. Cover: 94th. Carl R. Baldwin, ed. Racine, Wisc.: Western Printing and Lithographing Co., [1946?]. 155 pp., embossed blue hardcover with gold printing, 31.1 x 23.5 cm, photos, ports., map, roster. Dornbusch 1950: 1135, Smith: 10027, Zeigler: 1438. NSP, NYPL, SMPH.

Number 95

550 *The Cruise Record of the 95th United States Naval Construction Battalion, April 1943–September 1945. Published by and for the Battalion Personnel: A Record of Achievement.* Cover: Cruise Record, 95th Naval Construction Battalion. Anon. Chicago: Rogers Printing Co., [1945?]. 213 pp., embossed blue hardcover with gold printing and multicolor logo, 31.5 x 24 cm, photos, ports., map, roster. Dornbusch 1950: 1136, Smith: 10028. NYPL, SMPH.

Number 96

551 *96th Seabeeography.* Cover: 96 United States Naval Construction Battalion. Anon. Baton Rouge: Army & Navy Pictorial Publishers, [1946?]. 150 pp., white hardcover with brown bird and red printing, 30.9 x 23.4 cm, photos, ports., roster. Dornbusch 1950: 1137, Smith: 10029, Zeigler: 1439. SMPH.

Number 99

552 *Ninety-ninth Naval Construction Battalion History Book.* Cover: 99. [R. J. Cole, ed.]. Anon. San Francisco: Schwabacher-Frey Co., [1946?]. 118 leaves, blue hardcover with gold logo, 31 x 22.5 cm, photos, ports., roster. Dornbusch 1950: 1138, Smith: 10030. NYPL, SMPH.

Number 100

553 *Century: 100th U.S. Naval Construction Battalion, Commissioned July 17, 1943.* Cover: Century World War II: 100th U.S. Naval Construction Battalion. Anon. Comdr. H. D. Cavin, CEC, USNR, publisher. N.p., [1945?]. 100 leaves, gray paper cover with white printing, 26.7 x 33.7 cm, photos, ports., roster. SMPH.

554 *Pictorial Review, U.S. Naval Construction Battalion Number 100, Philippine Island Edition, 1945, Volume 2.* Cover: Pictorial Review, U.S. Naval Construction Battalion Number 100. Anon. R. L. Holt, photographer. R. L. Volkman, publisher. Harrisburg, Pa.: J. Horace McFarland, [1946?]. 112 leaves, printed on one side of sheet only, embossed blue hardcover with gold printing, 22.5 x 28.5 cm, photos, Dornbusch 1951 supp.: 1525, Smith: 10031. NYPL, SMPH.

Number 101

555 *101 Battalion First Anniversary Issue: Bolts & Bullets, 6 July 1944* (cover). Anon. N.p., [1944?]. 42 pp., white paper cover with multiple photos and white and black printing, 25.9 x 20 cm, photos, ports., roster. SMPH.

556 *A Stone's Throw From Tokyo: A Pictorial History of the 101st Seabees.* Cover: 101 Battalion, Bureau of Yards and Docks, Navy Dept. [A. J. Peterson and John Newall, Jr., eds.]. Chicago: Rogers Printing Co., [1945?]. 87 leaves, embossed brown hardcover with green and blue printing and decoration, 31 cm, photos, map, roster. Dornbusch 1950: 1139, Smith: 10032. NYPL, SMPH.

Number 102

557 *102 CB.* Cover: 102 Construction Battalion, "Second to None," 1943–1945. Anon. Baton Rouge: Army & Navy Pictorial Publishers, [1946?]. 186 pp., blue hardcover with gold-embossed printing, 30.8 x 23.5 cm, photos, ports., map, roster. Dornbusch 1950: 1140, Smith: 10033, Zeigler: 1440. SMPH.

Number 103

558 *103rd Construction Battalion Plaque.* Cover: Tour of Duty, 103 Naval Construction Battalion, 1943–1945. Anon. Baton Rouge: Army & Navy Publishing Co., [1946?]. 177 pp., embossed blue hardcover with gold printing, 30.8 x 23.4 cm, photos, roster. Dornbusch 1950: 1141, Smith: 10034. SMPH.

Number 105

559 *105 Naval Construction Battalion* (cover). Lester Colin. San Francisco: Crocker Union Co., [1945?]. 76 leaves, green hardcover with printing and tractor in gold, 27.9 x 20.8 cm, photos, ports., roster. Dornbusch 1950: 1142, Smith: 10035, Zeigler: 1441. NDL, SMPH, USNA.

Number 107

560 *The Log, 1943–1945: A Story of a Seabee Battalion Conceived in War, Dedicated to Peace, Published by 107th Naval Construction Battalion.* Cover: The Log of the 107 Seabees. Anon. Baton Rouge: Army & Navy Pictorial Publishers, [1946?]. 208 pp., embossed black hardcover with red and blue printing and decoration, 23 x 31 cm, photos, ports., map, roster. Dornbusch 1950: 1143, Smith: 10036, Zeigler: 1442. NYPL, SMPH.

Number 109

561 *1943–1944, CIX Annual.* Cover: 109. Anon. N.p., [1945?]. 129 pp., gray paper cover with shield in red, white, and blue, 23 x 31 cm, photos, ports., roster. Dornbusch 1950: 1144, Smith: 10037. SMPH.

Number 110

562 *"Contract Completed": Published by and for the Officers and Men of the 110th Naval Construction Battalion, 1943–1945.* Cover: "Contract Completed": 110th United States Naval Construction Battalion. Anon. Baton Rouge: Army & Navy Pictorial Publishers, [1946?]. 64 leaves, blue hardcover with gold printing and multicolor logo, 30.8 x 23.3 cm, photos, ports., roster. Dornbusch 1950: 1145, Smith: 10038. SMPH.

Number 111

563 *A Pictorial History of the 111 Naval Construction Battalion, 1943–1944.* Cover: 111: The One Hundred Eleventh Naval Construction Battalion. Anon. N.p., [1945?]. 145 pp., white hardcover with blue printing, 23.5 x 17.9 cm, photos, ports., roster. SMPH.

564 *History of the 111th U.S. Naval Construction Battalion, Depicting Its Activities in the Asiatic Pacific Theatre.* Anon. Los Angeles: Grimes Stratford Co., [1946?]. 59 leaves, blue hardcover with gold emblem, 28.7 x 22.3 cm, photos, ports., maps, roster. Dornbusch 1950: 1146, Smith: 10039. NDL, SMPH.

Number 112

565 Cover missing, no title page. Anon. N.p., [1945?]. 32 leaves, 29.2 x 22.6 cm, photos, ports., roster. SMPH.

Number 113

566 *The Story of the 113th Seabees: The Portrayal in Words and Pictures of a Naval Construction Battalion at Work and Play, From 5 August 1943 to 2 September 1945.* Anon. San Francisco: Schwabacher-Frey Co., 1947. 136 pp., blue hardcover with gold shield, 31.1 x 23.5 cm, photos, ports., map. NDL, SMPH.

Number 114

567 *The 114th U.S. Naval Construction Battalion.* Cover: 114 U.S. Naval Construction Battalion. Anon. N.p., [1946?]. 200 pp., embossed blue hardcover with gold printing and eagle, 27.3 x 20.2 cm, photos, ports., map, roster. NYPL, SMPH.

Number 115

568 *Naval Construction Battalion 115, 1943, 1944, 1945* (cover). Anon. Philadelphia: Edward Stern & Co., [1946?]. 80 leaves, tan hardcover with blue and red printing, 28.2 x 21.7 cm, photos, ports., roster. Dornbusch 1950: 1147, Smith: 10040. NDL, SMPH.

Number 116

569 *Work and Weapons: The Story of the One Hundred Sixteenth Naval Construction Battalion.* Cover: Work and Weapons. E. H. Melhorn and R. G. Westervelt, eds. Portland, Oreg.: James Kerns & Abbott Co., 1946. 111 pp., green hardcover with black, gold, and white printing and worker with sledge depicted, 28 x 21.8 cm, photos, ports., roster. Dornbusch 1950: 1148, Smith: 10041, Zeigler: 1443. NYPL, SMPH.

Number 117

570 *The Bulldog Travels.* Anon. N.p., [1945?]. 204 pp. Controvich 1992. No known copy location.

571 *The 117th Review, Anniversary Edition* (cover). Anon. Honolulu: Paradise of the Pacific, [1945?]. 55 pp., blue paper cover with white printing and photograph of sailors with flag, 29.8 x 21.8 cm, photos, ports., roster. Dornbusch 1950: 1149, Smith: 10042. SMPH.

Number 119

572 *Time Out: A Pictorial History of the 119th Seabees.* Cover: Time Out: 119th Seabees. Robert C. MacKicham and Hugh Shannon, eds. Worcester, Mass.: Davis Press, [1946?]. 221 pp., dust jacket, white hardcover with gold and blue printing and decoration, 27.3 x 21.7 cm, photos, ports., map, roster. Dornbusch 1950: 1150, Smith: 10043. NDL, SMPH.

Number 121

573 *Battalion History, May 10, 1943–August 15, 1945.* Cover: 121 CB. Mac McKerracher, Walt Frutiger, and Earl Yonkers, eds. Baton Rouge: Army & Navy Pictorial Publishers, [1946?]. 91 pp., blue hardcover with gold-embossed printing, 30.8 x 23.3 cm, photos, ports., roster. Dornbusch 1950: 1151, Smith: 10044, Zeigler: 1444. NDL, NYPL, SMPH.

Number 122

574 *Base Pacific, A History of the 122nd U.S. Naval Construction Battalion.* Cover: Base Pacific, the 122nd. Anon. N.p., [1945?]. 130 pp. plus pictorial section, blue hardcover with red and white printing, 31.9 x 23.3 cm, photos, ports., map, roster. Dornbusch 1950: 1152, Smith: 10045. SMPH.

Number 123

575 *123rd U.S. Naval Construction Batt. Year Book, Aug. 1943 to Jan. 1945, Win, Place, Show* (cover). [J. D. O'Laughlin, ed.]. N.p., [1945?]. 79 pp., 27.8 x 21.4 cm, photos, ports., roster. Dornbusch 1951: 1526, Smith: 10046. SMPH.

576 *Victory Year Book, 1945: 123, Win, Place, Show.* Cover: 123 United States Naval Construction Battalion. [Norman M. MacLeod, ed.]. Appleton, Wisc.: Petterson Press, 1946. 66 pp., blue hardcover with gold and red printing and Seabee logo, spiral binding, 31.3 x 23.8 cm, photos, ports., roster. Smith: 10046a. NYPL (rebound), SMPH.

Number 125

577 *Log Book, September 1943–November 1945: A Biography of the 125th U.S. Naval Construction Battalion.* Cover: 125 Log 1943–1945. Anon. New York: Robert W. Kelly Publishing Corp., [1946?]. 253 pp., brown hardcover with embossed title and multicolor shield, 31.2 x 23.6 cm, photos, ports., map, roster. Dornbusch 1950: 1153, Smith: 10047. NYPL, SMPH.

Number 128

578 *One Twenty-eighth USN. Construction Battalion (Pontoon), 1944–1945, Pacific Offensive* (cover). Anon. Chicago: [1946?]. 101 pp., green and cream hardcover with green and silver printing, 31.3 x 23.7 cm, photos, ports., map, roster. Dornbusch 1950: 1154, Smith: 10048. SMPH.

Number 130

579 *One Hundred and Thirtieth United States Naval Construction Battalion.* Chaplain N. P. Jacobson. Baton Rouge: Army & Navy Publishing Co., [1945?]. 299 pp., blue hardcover with red and yellow logo, 31.8 x 23.6 cm, photos, ports., map, roster. Dornbusch 1950: 1155, Smith: 10049, Zeigler: 1445. SMPH.

Number 133

580 *Rain Makers Log From "Boot to Black Hell".* Cover: 133 Naval Construction Battalion, 1943–1945. Lt. D. H. Greenfield, CEC, USNR, et al., eds. Rochester: Leo Hart Co., [1945?]. 201 pp., embossed blue hardcover with gold printing and multicolor shield, 31.2 x 24 cm, photos, ports., map, roster. Dornbusch 1950: 1156, Smith: 10050. NYPL, SMPH.

Number 135

581 *The 135th U.S. Naval Construction Battalion Review.* Cover: The 135th Review, USNCB. [F. P. Organ, ed.]. [San Francisco: A. Carlisle & Co., 1946?]. 99 leaves, black hardcover with gold printing and decoration, 31.1 x 25.8 cm, photos, ports., roster. Dornbusch 1950: 1157, Smith: 10051, Zeigler: 1446. SMPH.

Number 136

582 *Photo Memories of Seabee Battalion, Published by and for the Men of 136 Yokosuka, Japan, October, 1945.* Anon. Tokyo: Dai Nippon Printing Co., [1946?]. 87 leaves, green cover with Japanese mountain scene pasted on, 36.4 x 30.9 cm, photos, ports., roster. Dornbusch 1950: 1158, Smith: 10052, Zeigler: 1447. SMPH.

Number 138

583 *138th Naval Construction Battalion Maintains Island "X".* Cover: On Island X. Anon. Seattle: Deers Press, [1945?]. 104 leaves, gray hardcover with red printing, 23.4 x 16.2 cm, photos, ports., roster. Dornbusch 1950: 1159, Smith: 10053. SMPH.

Number 140

584 *Down Atabrine Alley With the 140th Seabees, Published by the 140th Naval Construction Battalion as a Permanent Record of Their First Tour of Duty.* Cover: Down Atabrine Alley with the 140th Seabees. Anon. Baton Rouge: Army & Navy Pictorial Publishers, [1946?]. 155 pp., embossed green hardcover with black printing with tractor and palm trees in background, 30.8 x 23.4 cm, photos, ports., roster. Dornbusch 1950: 1160, Smith: 10054. SMPH.

Number 141

585 *141 U.S. Navy Construction Battalion.* Cover: Souvenir Muster Book, 141st U.S. Navy Construction Battalion, Sept. 1944. Anon. N.p., [1944?]. 96 pp., blue paper cover with dark blue printing, 22.3 x 14.3 cm, photos, ports., roster. Dornbusch 1950: 1161, Smith: 10055. SMPH.

Number 142

586 *Of Men and Might: Story of the 142nd Naval Construction Battalion, January 15, 1944–January 15, 1945* (cover). Anon. N.p., [1945?]. 92 pp., white paper cover with black printing and photograph, 30.3 x 22.3 cm, photos, ports., roster. Dornbusch 1950: 1162, Smith: 10056. SMPH.

587 *Philippine Assignment, 142nd U.S. Naval Construction Battalion, May–Sept. 45.* Cover: Philippine Assignment, 142nd U.S. Naval Construction Battalion. Anon. N.p., [1945?]. 53 pp., brown hardcover (slightly flexible) with green printing, 31 x 23.2 cm, photos, map. SMPH.

Number 143

588 *143rd Naval Construction Battalion (Advance Base Construction Depot): A Battalion Biography.* Cover: 143rd NCB ABCD. Ens. S. W. Clark, ed. New York: Robert W. Kelly Publishing Corp., [1946?]. 254 pp., embossed blue hardcover with gold printing, 27.5 x 20.8 cm, photos, ports., roster. Dornbusch 1950: 1163, Smith: 10057, Zeigler: 1448. NDL, SMPH.

Number 145

589 *Service Record of the 145th Naval Construction Battalion, 1943–1944–1945.* Cover: Service Record, 145 Seabees. Anon. Baton Rouge: Army & Navy Pictorial Publishers, [1946?]. 290 pp., blue hardcover with gold title and medallion, 30.8 x 23.6 cm, photos, ports., map, roster. Dornbusch 1950: 1164, Smith: 10058. SMPH.

Number 147

590 *147 NCB.* Lt. (jg) Jason P. Moore, ed. Baton Rouge: Army & Navy Pictorial Publishers, 1946. 69 leaves, embossed blue hardcover with white printing and multicolor decoration, 31 x 23.5 cm, photos, ports., map, roster. Dornbusch 1951 supp.: 1528, Smith: 10059. NYPL.

Number 301

591 *301st U.S. Naval Construction Battalion, April 1944 to December 1945.* Cover: Pictorial Record, 301st U.S. Naval Construction Battalion. Anon. N.p., [1946?]. 247 pp., blue hardcover with gold printing and emblem, 23.5 x 31 cm, photos, ports., map, roster. Dornbusch 1950: 1165, Smith: 10060, NDL, SMPH.

Number 302

592 *302 Naval Construction Battalion: A Picture Story of Our Part in Eight Major Invasions.* Cover: 302 Naval Construction Battalion. Anon. San Francisco: Crocker Union, [1945?]. 106 leaves, blue hardcover with gold printing and star, 31.2 x 23.1 cm, photos, ports., roster. Dornbusch 1950: 1166, Smith: 10061. NYPL, SMPH.

Special Naval Construction Battalions

Battalions are numbered 1 through 38, and 41.

Number 4

593 *Our First Tour of Duty: 4th Special United States Naval Construction Battalion, January 20, 1943–November 7, 1944.* Cover: 4th Special Battalion. D. C. Boudreau, CY, ed. Berkeley: Lederer Street & Zeus Co., [1945?]. 24 leaves, blue hardcover with map of Guadalcanal and gold printing, 20.6 x 27.3 cm, photos, ports., roster. Dornbusch 1950: 1167, Smith: 9928. NYPL (rebound), private collection.

594 *Second Cruise Book, Fourth Special United States Naval Construction Battalion.* Cover: 4th Special Naval Construction Battalion. Anon. Baton Rouge: Army & Navy Pictorial Publishers, [1946?]. 24 leaves, embossed blue hardcover with gold printing, 27.1 x 19.5 cm, photos, ports., map, roster. Dornbusch 1951: 1529, Smith: 9928. NDL, SMPH.

Number 5

595 *The Story of the Fifth Special Naval Construction Battalion.* Cover: Contrast. [John G. Almutt, ed.]. N.p., [1945?]. 151 pp., embossed maroon cover with yellow printing, 27.4 x 20.4 cm, photos, ports., map, roster. Dornbusch 1950: 1168, Smith: 9930. NDL, SMPH, USNA.

Number 6

596 *Sixth Special U.S. Naval Construction Battalion, C/D Detachment: Tour of the Pacific, 1943–1945*. Anon. N.p., 1945. Paged by chapters, 42 leaves, brown paper cover, 19.7 x 15 cm, roster, list of functions. SMPH.

Number 8

597 *Eighth Special U.S. Naval Construction Battalion Section III, 1943–1945* (cover). Anon. San Francisco: Schwabacher-Frey Co., [1946?]. 36 leaves, heavy brown and white paper cover with white and brown printing and view of mountain in background, 21.3 x 27 cm, photos, ports., roster. NYPL, SMPH.

598 *Yearbook, First Anniversary Overseas, 1944: Eighth Special U.S. Naval Construction Battalion, Second Section*. Cover: 8th Special Stevedore. Anon. N.p., [1944?]. 44 pp., heavy gray paper cover with blue printing and decoration, 27.3 x 21.3 cm, photos, ports., map, roster. Dornbusch 1950: 1170, Smith: 9933. SMPH.

599 *On the Ball: Eighth Special Battalion, Second Section* (cover). Anon. N.p., [1943?]. 60 pp., plus mounted photo section, heavy blue paper cover with flying eagle over a globe in black printing, 26.6 x 19 cm, typewritten with printing on one side of page only, photos, roster. Dornbusch 1950: 1169. NYPL, SMPH.

Number 9

600 *First Cruise of the Ninth Special* (cover). Lt. Comdr. J. E. Kane, ed. Lt. Comdr. R. R. Bennett, publisher. N.p., December 1945. 139 pp., embossed blue hardcover with gold printing, 31.1 x 23.8 cm, photos, ports., roster. Dornbusch 1950: 1171, Smith: 9934. NYPL, SMPH.

Number 10

601 *10th Special U.S. Naval Construction Battalion, Stevedores, Second Section* (cover). MM3c William G. Baechle, Jr., USNR, ed. Exeter, Eng.: W. Chudley and Sons, [1945?]. 14 leaves, heavy cream paper cover with black and blue printing and with Seabee logo and silhouette of ship, 26.4 x 20.3 cm, photos, ports., roster. Dornbusch 1950: 1172, Smith: 9935. NYPL, SMPH.

Number 12

602 *U.S. Navy 12th "Boxcar Battalion" Special Battalion.* Cover: Saga of the 12th Special United States Naval Construction Battalion. PhoM2c R. M. Carner and Lt. John Louis Jones. Lt. (jg) P. L. Perrin, ed. 12th U.S. Naval Construction Battalion (Special), publisher. N.p., [1945?]. 60 leaves, red hardcover with gold printing, 31.2 x 23.5 cm, photos, ports., map, roster. NYPL, SMPH.

Number 16

603 *16th NCB Special: Anytime, Anywhere, Our Booms Span the World* (cover). Anon. N.p., [1945?]. 34 leaves, printed on one side of sheet only, flexible blue cover with silver printing, 21 x 34.7 cm, photos, ports., roster. Dornbusch 1950: 1173, Smith: 9942. SMPH.

Number 17

604 *Overseas Photo Record, 17th Spec. N.C.B., 1944–1945.* Cover: Overseas Photo Record, Seventeenth Special United States Naval Construction Battalion. Maurice Broun. N.p., 1945. 59 pp., blue hardcover with red printing and map in background, 36 x 45 cm, photos. SMPH.

Number 18

605 *Cruise Book, Eighteenth Special Naval Construction Battalion.* Lt. L. W. Hallenbeck, ed. Peleliu, [1945?]. 29 leaves, printed on one side of sheet, 20 x 27 cm, photos, map, roster. Dornbusch 1950: 1174, Smith: 9944. NYPL (film), SMPH.

Number 20

606 *The Manus Review, edited by Don Owen, Published by 20th Special U.S. Naval Construction Battalion.* Cover: 20th Special U.S. Naval Construction Battalion, 1943–1945. Don Owen, ed. Baton Rouge: Army & Navy Pictorial Publishers, [1946?]. 53 leaves, blue hardcover with red and gold printing, 30.7 x 23.4 cm, photos, ports., roster. Dornbusch 1950: 1175, Smith: 9945. SMPH.

Number 26

607 *26th Special Naval Construction Battalion: A Pictorial Record.* Cover: 26th Special Naval Constr. Batt. Anon. N.p.: 26th Spec. NCB Print Shop, [1945?]. 53 leaves, gray hardcover with title and emblem in black and blue, loose-leaf binding, 31.6 x 24.2 cm, photos, ports., roster. SMPH, USNA.

Number 28

608 *28th Special Naval Construction Battalion Presents Cargo Soundings Album, April 1944 to November 1945.* Cover: 28th Special Naval Construction Battalion, Seabees. Y1c Irwin Brown and Cox Bernard L. Laufbaum, eds. Baton Rouge: Army & Navy Pictorial Publishers, 1946. 172 pp., embossed blue hardcover with gold printing and Seabee logo, 30.9 x 23.7 cm, photos, ports., map, roster. Dornbusch 1950: 1176, Smith: 9954. NYPL, SMPH.

Number 30

609 *30th Special U.S. Naval Construction Battalion, Section 1* (top of page 1). Cover: Thirtieth Special Seabees, Section 1. Lt. (jg) H. C. Clagett, CEC, USNR, ed. N.p., [1945?]. 16 leaves, heavy white paper cover with blue printing and Seabee logo, 29.1 x 23.7 cm, photos, ports. Dornbusch 1950: 1178. SMPH.

610 *The Boom Dozer: 30th Special Naval Construction Battalion.* William K. Johnson, CSK, ed. N.p., [1946?]. 144 pp., blue hardcover with gold printing, 27.4 x 20.2 cm, photos, roster. Dornbusch 1950: 1177, Smith: 9957, Zeigler: 1425. SMPH, USNA.

Number 31

611 *Coming Through: The Story of the Thirty-first Special Naval Construction Battalion.* Edwin G. Bennett. Tokyo: Dai Nippon Printing Co., [1946?]. 64 pp., heavy blue and brown paper cover with yellow and black printing and globe in center, 25.7 x 18.7 cm, photos, roster. Dornbusch 1950: 1179, Smith: 9959, Zeigler: 1121. NYPL (film), SMPH.

Number 33

612 *The Log 33rd U.S. Naval Construction Battalion (Special).* Cover: 33 Special Construction Battalion, USN: The Log 33rd Special Naval Construction Battalion. Y3c H. Hirschman, ed. N.p., 1945. 115 pp., light brown hardcover embossed with dark brown printing with shield in background, 27.5 x 21.2 cm, photos, ports., roster. SMPH.

Number 34

613 *Battalion Review: 34th Special Battalion, USN, 1944–1945* (cover). [Bob Elder, ed.]. Baton Rouge: Army & Navy Pictorial Publishers, [1946?]. 109 pp., embossed blue hardcover with gold printing and brown and cream shield, 30.8 x 23.3 cm, photos, ports., map, roster. Dornbusch 1950: 1180, Smith: 9963, Zeigler: 1426. NYPL, SMPH.

Number 35

614 *35th Special U.S. Naval Construction Battalion, Lt. Albert B. Herbold, Officer-in-Charge* (cover). Anon. N.p., [1946?]. 27 leaves, printed on one side of page only, brown hardcover with black printing, loose-leaf screw binding, 24.8 x 32.3 cm, photos. NYPL (film), SMPH. This book is composed almost entirely of photographs arranged four to a page.

Number 37

615 *The 37th NCB Special Presents a Pictorial Review of the Men and Officers of Our Battalion.* Lt. M. A. Brunning, ed. N.p., [1946?]. 44 leaves, photos, ports., roster. NYPL (film).

Naval Construction Battalions, Maintenance Units

Battalions are numbered from 501 through 636.

Number 503

616 *United States Naval Construction Battalion, Maintenance Unit 503.* Cover: C.B.M.U. 503: Beach Combings, 1943–45. Anon. San Diego: Arts & Crafts Press, [1945?]. 56 leaves, heavy flexible blue cover with gold printing and decoration, 29.2 x 39.8 cm, photos, ports., roster. Dornbusch 1950: 1181, Smith: 10063. NYPL, SMPH.

Number 510

617 *C*B*M*U* 510* (cover). EM3c Leroy D. Hall, ed. Lt. Charles T. Turner, CEC, USNR, publisher. N.p., [1945?]. 49 leaves, green hardcover with red printing, 27.4 x 20.6 cm, photos, ports., roster. SMPH.

Number 512

618 *C.B.M.U. 512, June 1943–August 1945, Alaska & the Philippines* (cover). Anon. Baton Rouge: Army & Navy Pictorial Publishers, [1946?]. 89 pp., embossed blue hardcover with gold printing, 30.9 x 23.3 cm, photos, ports., roster. Dornbusch 1950: 1182, Smith: 10064. SMPH.

Number 521

619 *U.S. Naval Construction Battalion Maintenance Unit No. 521: Its Tour of Duty on Tulagi, British Solomon Islands, Okinawa, South Pacific, C.B.M.U. No. 521.* Cover: CBMU 521: Arctics to Tropics. Anon. N.p., [1945?]. 40 leaves, green hardcover with gold printing, 31.4 x 23.5 cm, photos, ports., map, roster. Dornbusch 1950: 1183, Smith: 10065. SMPH.

Number 535

620 *Lens-Eye View: CBMU 535.* Fred L. Williams, CCM manager. Baton Rouge: Army & Navy Pictorial Publishers, [1946?]. 74 pp., blue hardcover with gold printing and camera emblem, 31 x 23.3 cm, photos, ports., roster. Dornbusch 1950: 1184, Smith: 10066, NDL, SMPH.

Number 536

621 *U.S. Naval Construction Battalion Maintenance Unit 536, Commissioned September 23, 1943: 1943–1944–1945.* Anon. N.p., [1945?]. 47 leaves, blue hardcover with gold printing, 26 x 17.9 cm, photos, ports., map, roster. Dornbusch 1950: 1185, Smith: 10067. SMPH.

Number 537

622 *Construction Battalion Maintenance Unit 537.* Cover: CBMU 537, 1944. [Bruce Lester, ed.]. Auckland, New Zealand: Abel Dykes, [1944?]. 53 pp., blue hardcover with gold printing, 26 x 18 cm, photos, ports., roster. Dornbusch 1950: 1186, Smith: 10068. SMPH.

Number 540

623 *CBMU 540.* Cover: The Island X-quire: CBMU 540. Lt. Russell F. Hughes, CEC, USNR, ed. Lt. Comdr. John J. White, Jr., CEC, USNR, publisher. New York: F. Hubner & Co., [1946?]. 51 leaves, black hardcover with yellow printing, 31.2 x 23.4 cm, photos, ports., roster. SMPH.

Number 559

624 *The X-Isle Anniversary Edition, Vol. 1, No. 17* (cover). GM1c R. F. Melton, ed. Lt. A. E. Hilliard, publisher. N.p., Guardian Commercial Printery, December 15, 1944. 38 pp., beige cover with photograph of palm-lined island and black and white printing, 30.8 x 22.8 cm, photos, ports., roster. SMPH.

Number 561

625 *The 561st Log: A History in Picture and Story*. Cover: The 561 Log, 1943–45. Y1c Harry Zunger, ed. Chicago: Rogers Printing Co., [1946?]. 87 pp., blue hardcover with gold printing and decoration, 27.4 x 20.3 cm, photos, ports., roster. Dornbusch 1950: 1187, Smith: 10069. NYPL, SMPH.

Number 563

626 *CBMU 563: Courage, Teamwork, Leadership* (cover). Anon. N.p., [1945?]. 24 leaves, white paper cover with white printing on blue shield, 30.3 x 23 cm, photos, ports., roster. Private collection.

Number 571

627 *Can Do; Did: United States Naval Construction Battalion Maintenance Unit 571*. Cover: Can Do; Did: CBMU 571. Carl E. Johnson, ed. Chester J. Held, advisor. Duluth: Blewett Printing Co., [1946?]. 33 leaves, embossed blue hardcover with silver and gold printing and tractor, 31.2 x 23.4 cm, photos, ports., map, roster. Dornbusch 1950: 1188, Smith: 10062. SMPH.

Numbers 572 and 573

628 *Bitter Bellies*. Cover: Bitter Bellies: CBMU 572, CBMU 573, 1944–1945. Robert E. Stansfield, ed. Portland, Oreg.: Beattie and Hoffmann Printers, 1946. 145 pp., blue hardcover with gold printing, 20.9 x 15.2 cm, photos, ports., map, roster. SMPH.

Number 591

629 *Photo Log, C.B.M.U. No. 591*. Cover: Photo Log, C.B.M.U. No. 591, 1944–1945. BM2c L. G. Frankau, ed. N.p., [1945?]. 58 leaves, blue hardcover with silver printing, 24 x 31.5 cm, photos, ports., roster. Dornbusch 1950: 1189, Smith: 10070. SMPH.

Number 597

630 *First Anniversary, U.S. Naval Construction Battalion Maintenance Unit No. 597, First March 1945*. [W. F. Jackson, ed.]. Anon. Estes Park, Colo.: Estes Park Trail, 1945. 23 leaves, blue softcover with gold shield, 21.5 x 28 cm, photos, ports., roster. Dornbusch 1950: 1190, Smith: 10071. SMPH.

Number 599

631 *CB Annual 599* (cover). D. A. Alworth, ChC, ed. N.p., [1945?]. 166 pp., orange softcover with black printing and view of tractor working under palm trees, 28 x 22 cm, photos, ports., roster. Dornbusch 1950: 1191, Smith: 10072. SMPH.

Number 606

632 *C.B.M.U. 606: Build, Maintain, Defend Camp Parks, California; Camp Rousseau, California; Gamadodo, New Guinea; Lingayen Gulf; Luzon, P.I.; Clark Field, Luzon, P.I., 11 June 1944–2 Sept. 1945*. Cover: CBMU 606. SK1c Sherwood R. Hughs, ed. St. Louis, Mo.: Von Hoffman Printing Co., [1946?]. 40 leaves, embossed blue hardcover with gold printing, 31 x 23.2 cm, photos, ports., roster. Dornbusch 1950: 1192, Smith: 10073. NYPL, SMPH.

Number 610

633 *C.B.M.U. 610* (cover). Anon. Chicago: [1945?]. 111 pp., black hardcover with gold printing and Seabee logo, 28.8 x 22.4 cm, photos, ports., map, roster. Dornbusch 1950: 1193, Smith: 10074. SMPH.

Number 611

634 *611 * CBMU*. Cover: 611 * CBMU: A Brief History. Anon. N.p., [1945?]. 23 leaves, blue softcover with silver printing, 26.5 x 19 cm, photos, ports., map, roster. SMPH.

Number 621

635 *The Manus-Script*. Cover: The CBMU, No. 621: Manus-Script, 1944–1945. SKD1c L. G. Fitzpatrick. Baton Rouge: Army & Navy Pictorial Publishers, [1946?]. 95 pp., blue hardcover with gold printing, 30.8 x 23.3 cm, photos, ports., roster. Dornbusch 1950: 1194. SMPH.

Number 633

636 *C.B.M.U. 633 Okinawa* (cover). Anon. N.p., [1946?]. 25 leaves, printed on one side of sheet only, cover shows view of quonset hut under trees, 27.5 x 20.5 cm, photos, ports., map, roster. SMPH (photocopy).

Number 635

637 *CBMU 635: Seabees* (cover). Ralph G. Hewlett, ChC, ed. Baton Rouge: Army & Navy Pictorial Publishers, [1946?]. 143 pp., embossed blue hardcover with gold printing, 22.9 x 30.4 cm, photos, ports., map, roster. Dornbusch 1950: 1195, Smith: 10075, Zeigler: 1449. SMPH.

Naval Construction Battalion Detachments

These units are numbered from 1001–1095, 1101–1109, 1151–1163, and 3001.

Number 1008

638 *1008 Seabee Detachment, 1008 Construction Battalion Detachment, Tour of Duty, Solomon Islands, July 1943–May 1945*. Cover: 1008 Seabee Detachment. Anon. [Berkeley: Lederer Street and Zeus, 1946.] 114 pp., brown hardcover with blue printing and map of Solomon Islands in background, 26.4 x 33.8 cm, photos, ports., roster. Controvich 1992. SMPH.

Number 1011

639 *1011–Det. "Seabees," United States Amphibious Training Base, Ft. Pierce, Fla.* Anon. N.p., [1946?]. 75 leaves, 26 cm, photos, ports. Dornbusch 1950: 1196, Smith: 10076. No known copy location.

Number 1029

640 *The Ten Twenty-niner*. SK3c Sam Rosen, ed. Comdr. Ralph Bryan, CEC, USNR, publisher. Auckland, New Zealand: Whitcomb & Tombes, [1945?]. 96 pp., yellow paper cover with blue printing, 28.6 x 22.4 cm, photos, ports., roster. Dornbusch 1950: 1197, Smith: 10077. NYPL, SMPH.

Number 1049

641 *1049th Seabees, U.S. Naval Construction Detachment Transportation Unit* (cover). MM1c William R. Stagg, ed. Exeter, Eng.: W. Chudley & Son, [1945?]. 19 leaves, heavy blue paper cover with black printing and decoration of anchor and truck, 27.3 x 21 cm, photos, ports., map, roster. Dornbusch 1950: 1198, Smith: 10078. NYPL, SMPH.

Number 1050

642 *This Is CBD 1050.* Cover: CBD 1050. Anon. Baton Rouge: Army & Navy Pictorial Publishers, 1946. 138 pp., blue hardcover with gold-embossed title with emblem, 29.9 x 23.5 cm, photos, ports., map, roster. Dornbusch 1950: 1199, Smith: 10079, Zeigler: 1450. NDL, SMPH, USNA.

Number 1058

643 *First Arctic Oil Expedition, N.C.B.D. 1058, U.S.N.R.* Cover: Com-Ice-Pac Reports: CBD 1058. Lt. Harry F. Corbin, ed. Wichita: Grit Printing Co., [1945?]. 178 pp., blue and white hardcover with white printing and oil rig on snow field, 27.5 x 21 cm, photos, ports., map, roster. Dornbusch 1951: 1530, Smith: 10080. NYPL, SMPH.

Number 1067

644 *The Saga of 1067.* Cover: 1067th NCBU, Commissioned 14 Oct. 1944. L. H. Washburn, CBU, and Y3c F. E. Petters, eds. Baton Rouge: Army & Navy Pictorial Publishers, 1946. 103 pp., embossed blue hardcover with embossed printing and multicolor shield, 30.9 x 23.3 cm, photos, ports., map, roster. Dornbusch 1950: 1200, Smith: 10081. NYPL, SMPH.

Other Seabee Units

Acorn 51

645 *A Pictorial Record of the Activities of Acorn Fifty-one, United States Navy, January 19, 1945–October 5, 1945.* Cover: Acorn 51, United States Navy. Lt. (jg) E. V. Carey, ed. Philadelphia: Masterprint Campus Publishing, 1946. 58 pp., brown hardcover with gold printing, 28.8 x 22.2 cm, photos, ports., roster. SMPH.

Advance Base Construction Depot

646 *ABCD.* Lt. William W. Olmstead, officer-in-charge. N.p., 1945. 69 leaves, flexible blue cover without printing, spiral binding, 30.5 x 24 cm, photos, ports., roster. SMPH.

Camp Endicott, Rhode Island

647 *Camp Endicott, Naval Construction Training Center, Davisville, Rhode Island, Seabees* (cover). Anon. Baton Rouge: Army & Navy Publishing Co., [1946?]. 121 pp., embossed blue hardcover with gold printing and multicolor Seabee logo, 30.8 x 23.3 cm, photos, ports., roster. SMPH.

Camp Parks, California

648 *Camp Parks, Shoemaker, California, Seabees* (cover). Anon. Baton Rouge: Army & Navy Publishing Co., [1945?]. 57 pp., gray softcover with blue printing and Seabee logo, 22.5 x 30 cm, photos, ports. SMPH.

649 *Station Force Construction Battalion Replacement Depot, Camp Parks, Shoemaker, California* (cover). Anon. Baton Rouge: Army & Navy Publishing Co., [1945?]. 95 pp., embossed blue hardcover with gold printing, 30.9 x 23.3 cm, photos, ports., roster. SMPH.

Camp Peary, Virginia

650 *From Selectees to Seabees: Camp Peary, U.S.N.C.T.C., Captain J. G. Ward, U.S.N., Commanding Officer* (cover). Anon. Washington: U.S. Government Printing Office, 1943. 12 leaves, white paper cover with black printing, photos. SMPH.

Pontoon Assembly Detachment 3

651 *The Story of PAD 3, Pontoon Assembly Detachment.* Lt. (jg) Theron Alexander, Jr., and Lt. (jg) Norman B. Sanneman. N.p., [1946?]. 43 leaves, cover with black and white printing showing sailor blowing bugle, 26 x 21.8 cm, photos, officer roster. SMPH.

4

Other Naval Command Books

Amphibious Forces

Advanced Amphibious Base, Salcombe, England

652 *United States Navy Advanced Amphibious Base, Salcombe, 1943–1945* (cover). Lt. Frank Dearing and Lt. (jg) Fred M. Kirby II. Kingbridge, Devon, Eng.: J. R. Gill & Son, [1945?]. 14 leaves, white paper cover with red printing and blue photo of base, 23.3 x 17.8 cm, photos, ports. SMPH.

Amphibious Receiving Base, Plymouth, England

653 *Plymouth: United States Naval Amphibious Receiving Base, 1943–1945*. Anon. Philadelphia: N.p., [1945?]. 42 pp., 28 cm, photos, Dornbusch 1950: 1067, Smith: 9309. No known copy location.

Amphibious Training Command, Atlantic Fleet

654 *The Amphibs: Amphibious Training Command, United States Atlantic Fleet* (cover). Anon. Atlanta: Albert Love Enterprises, [1946?]. 30 leaves, paper cover with red and white lettering and color photograph of tank landing from *LST 547*, 30.4 x 22.5 cm, photos, ports. Private collection. This book shows activities at Camp Bradford, U.S. Naval Amphibious Training Base, Little Creek, Virginia; and Fort Pierce, Alabama.

Amphibious Training Command, Pacific Fleet

655 *PhibsTraPac: The Story of the Amphibious Trainee Training Command Amphibious Forces—Pacific Fleet* (cover). Anon. Atlanta: Albert Love Enterprises, [1946?]. 59 leaves, multicolor softcover showing soldier at the controls of vehicle, 29.9 x 22.2 cm, photos, ports. NDL.

Naval Landing Force Equipment Depot, Albany, California

656 *Naval Landing Force Equipment Depot, Albany, California*. Baton Rouge: Army & Navy Publishing Co., n.d. Army & Navy Publishing Co. List. No known copy location.

Naval Landing Force Equipment Depot, Norfolk, Virginia

657 *Anchors Aweigh*. Cover: Naval Landing Force Equipment Depot, Norfolk, Virginia. Anon. Baton Rouge: Army & Navy Publishing Co., [1945?]. 116 pp., blue hardcover with gold printing and decoration, 30.8 x 23.3 cm, photos, ports. NDL.

7th Amphibious Force

658 *7th Amphibious Force: Leyte, Lingayen, Morotai, Lae, Arawe, Corregidor, Gloucester, Hollandia* (cover). Anon. N.p., [1945?]. 32 leaves, buff paper cover with black printing and LST landing scene, 19.8 x 26.8 cm, photos, ports. Dornbusch 1950: 1066, Zeigler: 1419. NDL, NYPL.

Coast Guard Units

Coast Guard (general)

659 *"They Have to Go Out . . . But They Don't Have To Come Back".* United States Coast Guard. N.p., [1945?]. 40 pp., multicolor heavy paper cover with illustration, 28.4 x 41.6 cm, photos. USCGPA. This book covers Coast Guard wartime activities in general.

Coast Guard Auxiliary, Camden, New Jersey

660 *Wartime History of Flotilla No. 25, 1942–1945*. Ens. (T) John T. Dwyer, USCGR. N.p., [1946?]. 165 pp., blue hardcover with gold printing, 20.3 x 14 cm, photos, ports., roster. USCGA.

Coast Guard Flotilla 1–412

661 *The Battle of Boston Harbor: A Wartime History of Flotilla 1–412 Winthrop, Massachusetts*. CGM(T) John H. Fenton, USCGR. Published by author, 1946. 55 pp., blue hardcover with gold printing, 23.4 x 15.9 cm, photos, ports., roster. Controvich 1992. USCGA.

Coast Guard Philadelphia Regiment Volunteer Port Security Force

662 *The History of the Philadelphia Regiment Volunteer Port Security Force*. Lt. John F. Gummere, USCGR. Philadelphia: International Printing Co., 1946. 156 pp. plus 24 pp. of photos, blue softcover with gold printing and shield, 22.8 x 15.2 cm, photos, ports., officer roster. Smith: 9267. USCGA.

Coast Guard Recruiting Station, 3rd Naval District, Ellis Island, New York

663 *The Coast Guard on Ellis Island*. Frank K. Costa, ed. New York: Academy Photo Offset Inc., [1946?]. 44 leaves, light blue hardcover with dark blue printing of Coast Guard emblem, 28.5 x 22.4 cm, photos, ports. USCGPA.

Coast Guard SPARs

664 *Three Years Behind the Mast: The Story of the United States Coast Guard SPARs*. Lt. Mary C. Lyne, USCGR(W) and Lt. Kay Arthur, USCGR(W). Washington: N.p., [1946?]. 126 pp., tan and blue soft-cover with red and white printing, 22.8 x 15.1 cm, photos, ports. Controvich 1992. USCGA.

Coast Guard Temporary Reserve, 1st Naval District, Boston, Massachusetts

665 *The Coast Guard's TRs First Naval District*. Malcolm F. Willougby. Boston: Charles E. Louriat Co., 1945. 247 pp. Controvich 1992. No known copy location.

Coast Guard Temporary Reserve 5A, 1st Naval District, Boston, Massachusetts.

666 *Reminiscences of Your Hitch in the United States Coast Guard During World War II, 1941–1945: A Pictorial Record of USCG Temporary Reserve Activities in Division 5A, First Naval District*. Cover: Temporary Reserve, Division 5A—First Naval District. Clifton A. Follansbee, ed. Boston: December 1946. 96 pp., blue hardcover with gold printing and gold Coast Guard emblem, 23.3 x 29.7 cm, photos, ports., map. Smith: 9250. USCGA.

Coast Guard Temporary Reserve, 13th Naval District, Seattle, Washington

667 *Norwester: Annual Edition, 1945*. Cover: Norwester. Ens. Dan P. Cheney, ed. Claude Walter, publisher. Seattle: 1945. 139 pp., multicolor hardcover with U.S. and Coast Guard flags and gold printing, 27.5 x 21.4 cm, photos, ports., map, rosters. Private collection.

Coast Guard Training Station, Atlantic City, New Jersey

668 *U.S. Coast Guard Training Station, Atlantic City, New Jersey*. Baton Rouge: Army & Navy Publishing Co., n.d. Army & Navy Publishing Co. List. No known copy location.

Coast Guard Training Station, Fort McHenry, Maryland

669 *U.S. Coast Guard Training Station, Fort McHenry, Maryland*. Cover: The Vulcan Log, United States Coast Guard Fort McHenry, Maryland. Anon. Baton Rouge: Army & Navy Publishing Co., [1946?]. Army & Navy Publishing Co. List. 30 leaves, embossed blue hardcover with gold printing and emblem, 30.7 x 23 cm, photos, ports., rosters. USCGA.

Coast Guard Training Station, Groton, Connecticut

670 *U.S. Coast Guard Training Station, Groton, Connecticut.* Cover: U.S. Coast Guard Training Station, Groton, Conn., 1944, United States Coast Guard 1790. Anon. Baton Rouge: Army & Navy Publishing Co., 1944. 84 pp., embossed blue hardcover with gold printing and shield, 30.8 x 23.3 cm, photos, ports., roster. Army & Navy Publishing Co. List. USCGA.

U.S. Coast Guard Academy, New London, Connecticut

671 *1940 Tide Rips.* Cover: Tide Rips. Joseph James McClelland and William Kehr Earle, eds. Buffalo, N.Y.: Baker Jones Hausauer Inc. (printer), The Corps of Cadets of the USCG Academy, 1940. 221 pp., black hardcover with black printing and shield, 31 x 23.5 cm, photos, ports., senior roster. USCGA.

672 *1941 Tide Rips: The Yearbook of the Cadet Corps of the United States Coast Guard Academy.* Cover: Tide Rips. Whitney Matthews Prall, Jr., and John Stan, eds. Buffalo, N.Y.: Baker Jones Hausauer Inc. (printer), 1941. 207 pp., embossed blue hardcover with gold printing and ship silhouette, 31 x 23.8 cm, photos, ports., senior roster. USCGA.

673 *1942 Tide Rips 1943, United States Coast Guard Academy.* Cover: Tide Rips 1942–1943. Kenneth E. Wilson, ed. Rochester, N.Y.: Leo Hart Co. (printer), 1943. 285 pp., embossed brown hardcover with gold printing, 31 x 24 cm, photos, ports., senior roster. USCGA.

674 *Tide Rips 1944: The Annual Publication of the Corps of Cadets, United States Coast Guard Academy, New London, Connecticut.* James P. Van Etten, ed. N.p., 1944. Blue and gray hardcover with embossed gold eagle emblem, 31.8 x 24.3 cm, photos, ports., senior roster. USCGA.

675 *Tide Rips 1945: The Annual Publication of the Corps of Cadets, United States Coast Guard Academy, New London, Connecticut.* Cover: U.S. Coast Guard Academy. Anon. New York: Hibbert Printing Co., 1945. 275 pp., embossed blue hardcover with gold emblem, 31.2 x 24 cm, photos, ports., senior roster. USCGA.

676 *Tide Rips: Chronicles the Parade of Events During Our Three Years As Cadets at the United States Coast Guard Academy, New London, Connecticut, Class of 1946.* Anon. New York: Hibbert Printing Co., 1946. 266 pp., embossed blue hardcover with gold printing and shield, 31.2 x 23.7 cm, photos, ports., senior roster. USCGA.

Naval Medical Facilities

Fleet Hospital 103

677 *Fleet Hospital 103*. Cover: Fleet Hospital 103, Guam, 1945. [Stella Strickland, ed.] Anon. N.p., 1945. 124 pp., embossed blue hardcover with green printing, 31 x 23.5 cm, photos, ports., roster. BMA, NDL.

Fleet Hospital 105

678 *U.S. Fleet Hospital 105*. Anon. Auckland, New Zealand: Abel Dykes, Christmas, 1944. 20 leaves, blue hardcover with gold printing and cross decoration, 26 x 18.2 cm, photos, ports. NDL.

Fleet Hospital 115

679 *United States Fleet Hospital No. 115, Built by 48th N.C.B. and Hospital Staff, Commissioned 7 Dec. 1944, Completed 1 April 1945*. Cover: Fleet Hospital 115, Guam. Anon. Philadelphia: George Fein & Co., [1946?]. 136 pp., blue hardcover with gold printing, 28.7 x 22.5 cm, photos, ports., map, roster. BMA.

Naval Base Hospital Number 3

680 *Naval Base Hospital No. Three, Espirito Santo, New Hebrides*. Lt. Comdr. Murray W. Shulman, MC, USNR, et al., eds. N.p., 1944. 27 leaves, blue hardcover with gold shield, 22 x 28.3 cm, photos, ports., roster. BMA.

Naval Base Hospital Number 12

681 *The Story of SNAG 56*. Henry W. Hudson. Cambridge, Mass.: Harvard University Press, 1946. 93 pp. plus illustration section. Dabney Catalogue 380, December 1991. Private collection.

Naval Base Hospital Number 18

682 *U.S. Naval Base Hospital No. 18, Commissioned November 18, 1944*. Cover: U.S. Naval Base Hospital No. 18, Guam, M.I. Anon. Baton Rouge: Army & Navy Pictorial Publishers, 1946. 92 pp., blue hardcover with gold-embossed printing, 30.7 x 23 cm, photos, ports., map, roster. Dornbusch 1950: 1068, Smith: 9842. BMA, NDL.

Naval Hospital, New Orleans, Louisiana

683 [Naval Hospital, New Orleans, Louisiana]. Baton Rouge: Army & Navy Publishing Co., [1946?]. Army & Navy Publishing Co. List. No known copy location.

Naval Hospital, St. Albans, New York

684 *A Pictorial Review of United States Naval Hospital, St. Albans, Long Island, N.Y.* Elwood W. Loveridge. Philadelphia: Campus Publishing Co., [1945?]. 16 leaves, blue softcover with gold printing and white decoration, 26.6 x 19.7 cm, photos, ports. BMA.

Naval Hospital, Shoemaker, California

685 *United States Naval Hospital, Shoemaker, California* (cover). Anon. Baton Rouge: Army & Navy Publishing Co., [1945?]. 80 pp., embossed blue hardcover with gold printing, 30.8 x 23 cm, photos, ports., roster. NDL.

Naval Mobile Hospital Number 8

686 *The Story of the U.S. Naval Mobile Hospital Number 8.* Cover: U.S.N. Mobile Hospital No. 8. Capt. William H. H. Turville, MC. New York: Robert W. Kelly Publishing Corp., [1945?]. 164 pp., blue hardcover with gold printing and emblem of cross in circle, 27.3 x 20.3 cm, photos, ports. Smith: 9840, Zeigler: 713. BMA.

Naval Receiving Hospital, San Francisco, California

687 *Anniversary Booklet.* Cover: U.S. Naval Receiving Hospital, December 1944–December 1945. PhM3c Charles Haynes and PhM3c Paul Manchese, eds. San Francisco: U.S. Naval Receiving Hospital, 1946. 31 leaves, blue hardcover with gold printing and decoration, 23.8 x 15.6 cm, photos, ports., roster. BMA.

Naval Special Hospital, Sun Valley, Idaho

688 *The Sun Valley Sage Farewell Edition, U.S. Naval Special Hospital, Sun Valley, Idaho* (cover). Lt. O. R. Barnes, ed. N.p., 1945. 29 pp., white softcover with blue printing and photograph of Sun Valley, 30.5 x 22.8 cm, photos, ports., roster. BMA.

Naval Special Hospital, Yosemite National Park, California

689 *U.S. Naval Special Hospital, Yosemite National Park, California.* Cover: History of the United States Naval Special Hospital, Yosemite National Park, California. Anon. Yosemite National Park: Yosemite Park and Curry Co., 1946. 76 pp., blue softcover with gold printing and decoration, 23.5 x 17.8 cm, photos, ports., roster. Zeigler: 712. BMA.

Officer Training

Naval Pre-Flight School, University of Pennsylvania, Philadelphia

690 *Presenting the Activities of the United States Naval Flight Preparatory School, Philadelphia, Pennsylvania.* Cover: U.S. Naval Flight Preparatory School, University of Pennsylvania, Philadelphia, Pa. Anon. Philadelphia: Hollander & Feldman Studios, 1943. 16 leaves, blue softcover with view of trainees at college and black and white printing, 27.8 x 21.5 cm, photos, ports. NDL.

Naval Reserve Midshipmen's School, New York, New York

691 *Pass in Review.* Anon. New York: Robert W. Kelly Publishing Corp., December 1945. 157 pp., embossed blue hardcover with gold printing and emblem, 27.7 x 21 cm, photos, ports. NDL.

692 *The Side Boy.* Anon. First Class United States Reserve Midshipmen's School, USS *Illinois*, publisher. N.p., 1940. 83 pp., embossed blue hardcover with gold printing and decoration, 27.6 x 20.2 cm, photos, ports., roster. NDL.

693 *Side Boy.* Cover (spine): Side Boy Oct. '42. R. C. Lewis, ed. Eighth Class United States Naval Reserve Midshipmen's School, publisher. New York: Robert W. Kelly Publishing Corp., 1942. 148 pp. including advertising section, embossed blue hardcover, 27.5 x 20.5 cm, photos, ports., roster. No known copy location.

694 *24th Class Administration Activities Midshipmen, United States Naval Reserve Midshipmen's School, New York.* Cover (spine): Side Boy July 1945. Robert W. Sedwick, ed. New York: Robert W. Kelly Publishing Corp., 1945. 223 pp. including advertising section, embossed blue hardcover with gold and silver shield on front and gold printing on spine, 27.3 x 20.4 cm, photos, ports., roster. No known copy location.

695 *Pass In Review.* Anon. New York: Robert W. Kelly Publishing Corp., December 1945. 157 pp. embossed blue hardcover with gold printing and emblem, 27.7 x 21 cm, photos, ports., NDL. With souvenir books published by four classes out of at least 25 classes, it is highly probable that souvenir books exist for other classes as well.

Naval Reserve Midshipmen's School, Northwestern University

696 *Abbott Hall U.S.N.R.: The Record of the United States Naval Reserve Midshipmen's School, Abbott Hall, Northwestern University, September 1940–August 1945*. Cover: Abbott Hall, USNR, 1940–1945. Anon. Chicago: Abbott Hall Publications Committee, 1945. 172 pp., blue hardcover with gold printing, 24.5 x 17.2 cm, photos, ports. Dornbusch 1950: 1065. NDL.

Naval Reserve Midshipmen's School, Notre Dame, Indiana

697 *The Capstan: Midshipmen's School, U.S. Naval Reserve, Notre Dame, Indiana*. Cover: Capstan. Anon. N.p., May 1943. 216 pp. plus advertising section, embossed blue hardcover with gold printing and capstan, 28 x 22 cm, photos, ports., roster. NDL.

698 *Capstan: U.S. Naval Reserve Midshipmen's School, Notre Dame, Indiana, September 1943*. Cover: Capstan. Richard C. Prosch, ed. South Bend: Peerless Press, September 1943. 229 pp. plus advertising section, embossed blue hardcover with gold printing and capstan decoration, 28 x 22 cm, photos, ports., roster. Private collection.

Naval Reserve Officers Training Corps, Duke University

699 *The Dolphin, 1945–1946*. William J. Farren, ed. N.p., 1946. 96 pp., embossed blue hardcover with white emblem, 28.6 x 22.2 cm, photos, ports., roster. NDL.

Naval Reserve Officers Training Corps, V–12 and V–5, Marquette University

700 *Porthole, June 1946: Presented by Marquette Naval Unit NROTC V–12, V–5*. Anon. N.p., June 1946. 96 pp., embossed blue hardcover with green printing, 29 x 22.6 cm, photos, ports. NDL.

Naval Reserve Officers Training Corps, Northwestern University

701 *The Purple Salvo, February 1946*. Anon. 19th Graduating Class of NROTC, Northwestern University, publisher. Evanston, Ill.: 1946. 68 pp., blue hardcover with gold printing and decoration, 27.5 x 20.5 cm, photos, ports., roster. NDL.

Naval Reserve Officers Training Corps, University of Minnesota, Minneapolis

702 *Gopher Log: United States Navy, University of Minnesota at Minneapolis.* Cover: Gopher Log USN. P. F. Koenigsberger, ed. N.p., 1943. 27 leaves plus advertising section, blue hardcover with gold printing and decoration, 28.5 x 22.2 cm, photos, ports., roster. NDL.

703 *Gopher Log: United States Navy, University of Minnesota at Minneapolis.* John F. Dablow, ed. N.p., 1944. 53 leaves plus advertising section, embossed blue hardcover with emblem, 28.8 x 22.3 cm, photos, ports., roster. NDL.

704 *The 1945 Gopher Log, 1945: Naval Reserve Officers Training Corps, University of Minnesota at Minneapolis.* Cover: The Gopher Log, 1945. Neil Ball, ed. N.p., Lund Press, 1945. 63 leaves plus 12 leaves of advertisements, embossed blue hardcover with gold printing and gold and silver shield, 28.7 x 22.5 cm, photos, ports., roster. Private collection.

Naval Reserve Officers Training Corps, University of New Mexico, Albuquerque

705 *The Drydock.* Cover: The Drydock, June 1946. J. Richard Primm, ed. USNROTC University of New Mexico, Albuquerque, publisher. N.p., June 1946. 46 leaves plus advertising section, embossed black hardcover with gold printing, 22.5 x 20.2 cm, photos, ports., roster. NDL.

Naval Reserve Officers Training Corps, University of North Carolina, Chapel Hill

706 *The Catapult: Annual Edition, March 1944, Vol. 4, No. 4.* Cover: NROTC Catapult 1944. F. G. Walt, ed. N.p., 1944. 72 pp., blue hardcover with gold printing and emblem, 27.5 x 20.3 cm, photos, ports., roster. NDL.

707 *United States Navy and the University of North Carolina Present the Catapult, The Senior Edition, February 1945—Vol. 5, No. 5.* Cover: Catapult 1945, NROTC. Albert Jacobson, ed. N.p., 59 leaves plus advertising section, embossed black hardcover with gold printing and emblem, 27.5 x 20.3 cm, photos, ports., roster. NDL.

Naval Reserve Officers Training Corps and V-12 Unit, Harvard University

708 *Navy R.O.T.C. and V–12 Unit, Harvard University, U.S. Naval Training Schools* (cover). Anon. Baton Rouge: Army & Navy Publishing Co., [1945?]. 68 pp., embossed blue hardcover with gold printing and emblem, 30.9 x 23.3 cm, photos, ports., roster. NDL.

Naval Training School, Dartmouth College, Hanover, New Hampshire

709 *United States Naval Training School, Dartmouth College, Hanover, New Hampshire, August 15–September 8, 1942*. Cover: United States Naval Training School. Anon. N.p., 1942. 78 pp., blue softcover with gold printing, 27.8 x 21.7 cm, ports., roster. NDL.

Navy Pre-Flight School, Chapel Hill, North Carolina

710 *Presenting the Activities of the United States Navy Pre-Flight School, Chapel Hill, North Carolina, 1942–1943*. Cover: U.S. Navy Pre-Flight School, Chapel Hill, North Carolina. Anon. Philadelphia: Merin Baliban Studios, 1943. 18 leaves, brown and white softcover with white printing and view of scout plane in clouds, 26.8 x 19.8 cm, photos, ports. PNAM.

Navy Pre-Flight School, St. Mary's, California

711 *The History of U.S. Navy Pre-Flight School, St. Mary's, California*. Anon. Berkeley: Lederer Street & Zeus Co., [1946?]. 216 pp., blue hardcover with gold printing and decoration, 22.9 x 30.5 cm, photos, ports. NDL.

Navy Pre-Flight School, University of Georgia, Athens, Georgia

712 *Cadet Life at United States Navy Pre-Flight School at Athens, Georgia*. Second edition. Cover: U.S. Navy Pre-Flight School, Athens, Georgia: Tomorrow We Fly. Anon. Philadelphia: Merin-Baliban Studios, [1944?]. 18 leaves, multicolor paper cover showing planes on carrier deck, 26.6 x 19.6 cm, photos, ports. PNAM, SCM.

Navy V–12 Program, Stevens Institute of Technology, Hoboken, New Jersey

713 *The Nineteen Forty-four Link*. Cover: The Nineteen Forty-four Link: Stevens Institute of Technology. Donald R. Yennie et al., eds. Junior Class, Stevens Institute of Technology, publisher. N.p., 1944. 176 pp., embossed blue hardcover with gold printing and emblem, 31.2 x 23.5 cm, photos, ports., roster. NDL.

U.S. Naval Academy, Annapolis, Maryland

714 *Lucky Bag: The Annual of the Regiment of Midshipmen.* Cover: The Lucky Bag, Nineteen Forty. William D. Lanier, Jr., ed. Buffalo, N.Y.: Baker, Jones, Hausauer, 1940. 562 pp., gray hardcover with picture of academy grounds and buildings in gray and green, 30.5 x 22.9 cm, photos, ports., roster. NDL, USNA.

715 *The Lucky Bag of the Class of 1941.* Cover: Lucky Bag Annapolis. John Landreth, ed. N.p.: Edwards and Broughton Co., 1941. 416 pp., royal blue hardcover with sailboat and seagull in white, 35.6 x 27.9 cm, photos, ports., roster. NDL, USNA.

716 *The 1942 Lucky Bag: The Annual of the Regiment of Midshipmen.* Cover: The Lucky Bag 1942. Richard W. Arey, ed. Buffalo, N.Y.: Baker, Jones, Hausauer, 1942. 519 pp., beige hardcover with black printing and photo of ship in black and white, 30.5 x 22.9 cm, photos, ports., roster. NDL, USNA.

717 *Lucky Bag 1943: The Day by Day Story of the Regiment of Midshipmen of the United States Naval Academy, Annapolis, Maryland.* Cover: Lucky Bag. Anon. Raleigh: Edwards and Broughton Co., 1943. 446 pp., blue hardcover with embossed red printing, 36.6 x 28.8 cm, photos, ports., roster. NDL, USNA.

718 *The 1944 Lucky Bag: The Annual of the Regiment.* Cover: The 1944 Lucky Bag. George Downes Prestwich, ed. Rochester, N.Y.: Leo Hart Co., 1944. 516 pp., blue hardcover with gold printing and gold sea goddess, 35.6 x 27.9 cm, photos, ports., roster. NDL, USNA.

719 *Nineteen Hundred and Forty-Five Lucky Bag: Centennial Edition.* Cover: U.S. Naval Academy Seal with 1845–1945. Thomas Weir Johnston, ed. 1945 Class of the Regiment of Midshipmen of USNA, publisher. Rochester, N.Y.: Leo Hart Co., 1945. 608 pp., embossed wine hardcover with gold numbers and Naval Academy Seal, 36.3 x 29.5 cm, photos, ports., roster. PNAM, USNA.

720 *The 1946 Lucky Bag: The Yearbook of the Regiment of Midshipmen of the United States Naval Academy.* Cover: 1946 Lucky Bag. Donald Grote, ed. The Regiment of Midshipmen, USNA, publisher. Baltimore: Thomsen-Ellis-Hutton Co., 1946. 599 pp., embossed blue hardcover with gold eagle, 36.3 x 28.9 cm, photos, ports., roster. NDL, USNA.

Supply Corps

Bureau of Supplies and Accounts

721 *History of the Bureau of Supplies and Accounts in World War II: A Synopsis*. Bureau of Supplies and Accounts. N.p., October 1946. 186 pp., bound, 26.9 x 20 cm. SCM. This is not a true cruise book but a history of the Bureau of Supplies and Accounts.

Naval Supply Corps Operational Training School, Lido Beach, New York

722 *Gold Leafings: Naval Supply Operational Training School, Lido Beach, Long Island, New York*. Cover: Gold Leafings, January 1945. L. B. Howard, ed. New York: H. R. Elliot, January 1945. 39 leaves, blue hardcover with gold and silver printing and decoration, 27.3 x 20.2 cm, photos, ports., roster. SCM.

Naval Supply Corps School, Babson Park, Massachusetts

723 *Navy Supply Corps School, Babson Unit, Specialists Class of July 1943, Babson Institute of Business Administration, Babson Park, Massachusetts*. Cover: Navy Supply Corps School, Babson Unit, July 1943. Anon. Andover, Mass.: Andover Press, 1943. 51 pp., blue hardcover with gold printing and decoration, 23.4 x 15.8 cm, photos, ports., roster. SCM.

724 *Navy Supply Corps School, Babson Unit, Specialists Class of August 1943, Babson Institute of Business Administration, Babson Park, Massachusetts*. Cover: Navy Supply Corps School, Babson Unit, Class of August 1943. Anon. Andover, Mass.: Andover Press, 1943. 32 pp., blue hardcover with gold printing and decoration, 27.2 x 20 cm, photos, ports., roster. SCM.

725 *Navy Supply Corps School, Babson Unit, Specialists Class of October 1943. Babson Institute of Business Administration, Babson Park, Massachusetts*. Anon. N.p., October 1943. 29 pp., photos, ports., roster. SCM (photocopy).

726 *Navy Supply Corps School, Babson Unit, Specialists Class of January 1944, Babson Institute of Business Administration, Babson Park, Massachusetts*. Cover: Navy Supply Corps School, Babson Unit, January 1944. Anon. N.p., January 1944. 32 pp., blue hardcover with gold printing and decoration, 27.1 x 20.2 cm, photos, ports., roster. SCM.

727 *Navy Supply Corps School, Babson Unit, Specialists Class of May 1944, Babson Institute of Business Administration, Babson Park, Massachusetts.* Cover: Navy Supply Corps School, Babson Unit, May 1944. Anon. Wellesley, Mass.: Wellesley Press, May 1944. 15 leaves, blue hardcover with gold printing and decoration, 27.2 x 20.1 cm, photos, ports., roster. SCM.

728 *Navy Supply Corps School, Class of August 1944, Babson Unit Specialists, Babson Institute of Business Administration, Babson Park, Massachusetts.* Cover: Navy Supply Corps School, Babson Unit Class of August 1944. Anon. N.p., August 1944. 18 leaves, blue hardcover with gold printing and decoration, 27.2 x 20.1 cm, photos, ports., roster. SCM.

729 *Navy Supply Corps School, Class of October 1944, Babson Unit Specialists, Babson Institute of Business Administration, Babson Park, Massachusetts.* Anon. Worcester, Mass.: The Stobb's Press, October 1944. 18 leaves, embossed blue hardcover with embossed eagle, 27.5 x 20.4 cm, photos, ports., roster. SCM. This book was issued in two states. The other version has a light blue cover with the following cover title: Navy Supply Corps School, Babson Unit, Class of October 1944.

Naval Supply Corps School, Bayonne, New Jersey

730 *Account Current: Naval Supply Corps School* (cover). Anon. October and December 1946 Classes of Naval Supply Corps School, publishers. N.p., December 1946. 55 leaves, blue hardcover with embossed title and gold decoration, 27.5 x 20.5 cm, photos, ports., roster. SCM. The Naval Supply Corps School was transferred from Harvard to Bayonne, New Jersey, on July 1, 1946.

Naval Supply Corps School, Harvard University, Cambridge, Massachusetts

731 *The Class Book: Navy Supply Corps School, 1941.* Cover: Navy Supply Corps School, Harvard University, 1941. L. A. Campbell, ed. Andover, Mass.: Andover Press, 1941. 96 pp., blue hardcover with gold printing and decoration, 23.5 x 15.7 cm, photos, ports., roster. SCM.

732 *The Navy Supply Corps School, Class of February, 1942.* Cover: Navy Supply Corps School, Harvard University, February 1942. S. M. Hess, ed. Boston: Warren Press, 1942. 79 pp., blue hardcover with gold printing and decoration, 23.7 x 15.8 cm, photos, ports., roster. SCM.

733 *The Yearbook of the Navy Supply Corps School, Soldiers Field Station, Boston, Massachusetts, July 1942.* Cover: Navy Supply Corps School, Harvard University, July 1942. Ens. Arthur E. Burdge, SC, USNR, ed. Boston: Warren Press, 1942. 91 pp., blue hardcover with gold printing and decoration, 27.3 x 20.5 cm, photos, ports., roster. NDL, SCM.

734 *The Yearbook of the Navy Supply Corps School.* Cover: Navy Supply Corps School, Harvard University, Summer—1942—Fall. Ens. M. Greely Summers, Jr., SC, USNR, ed. Boston: Warren Press, 1942. 88 pp., blue hardcover with green-gold printing and decoration, 27.2 x 20.3 cm, photos, ports., roster. SCM.

735 *The Yearbook of the Navy Supply Corps School.* Cover: Navy Supply Corps School, Harvard University, Fall 1942. Ens. Alfred Lorber, SC, USNR, ed. N.p., 1942. 95 pp., blue hardcover with gold printing and decoration, 27.2 x 20.3 cm, photos, ports., roster. SCM.

736 *The Rough Roll: Class Book of the Navy Supply Corps School, Winter 1943.* Cover: The Rough Roll, Harvard University, Winter—1943. E. M. McPherson, ed. N.p., 1943. 119 pp., white hardcover with blue printing and decoration, 27.3 x 20.5 cm, photos, ports., roster. SCM.

737 *The Rough Roll: A Classbook of the Navy Supply Corps School, Harvard University, Soldier's Field, Boston, Massachusetts.* Cover: The Rough Roll, Harvard University, May 1943. A. F. Conners, ed. N.p., May 1943. 134 pp., blue hardcover with gold printing and decoration, 27.2 x 25.3 cm, photos, ports., roster. SCM.

738 *The Rough Roll: The Accounts of the August 1943 Class of the Navy Supply Corps School, Harvard University.* Cover: The Rough Roll: Harvard University, August 1943. Alden C. Manchester, ed. N.p., 1943. 133 pp., blue hardcover with gold printing and decoration, 27.2 x 20.4 cm, photos, ports., roster. SCM.

739 *The Rough Roll: Classbook of the Navy Supply Corps School, Harvard University, Boston, Massachusetts.* Cover: The Rough Roll, Harvard University, October 1943. William N. Cassella, Jr., ed. N.p., October 1943. 103 pp., blue hardcover with gold printing and decoration, 27.3 x 20.3 cm, photos, ports., roster. SCM.

740 *The Rough Roll: Classbook of the Navy Supply Corps School, Harvard University, December 1943.* Cover: The Rough Roll, Harvard University, December 1943. F. Gordon Boyce, ed. N.p., December 1943. 151 pp., blue hardcover with gold printing and decoration, 27.2 x 20.5 cm, photos, ports., roster. SCM.

741 *The Memo: Navy Supply Corps Midshipmen Officers' School, Harvard Graduate School of Business Administration.* Cover: The Memo, January 1944: United States Navy Supply Corps Midshipmen—Officers' School, Harvard School of Business. Tod Stromquist, ed. Boston: Warren Press, January 1944. 32 leaves, blue hardcover with gold and black printing, 27.1 x 20.5 cm, photos, ports., roster. SCM.

742 *The Rough Roll: Classbook of the Navy Supply Corps School, Harvard University, March 1944.* Cover: The Rough Roll, Harvard University, March 1944. John E. Jackson, ed. N.p., March 1944. 119 pp., blue hardcover with gold printing and decoration, 27.5 x 20.9 cm, photos, ports., roster. SCM.

743 *The Rough Roll: Class Book of the Navy Supply Corps School, Harvard University, May 1944.* Cover: The Rough Roll: Harvard University, May 1944. E. K. Houser and H. M. Anderson, eds. Boston: Warren Press, May 1944. 116 pp., blue hardcover with gold printing and decoration, 27.2 x 20.5 cm, photos, ports., roster. SCM.

744 *The Golden Fleece: For He Was to Search for, of Universal Tranquility.* Cover: The Golden Fleece: NSCS Harvard, August '44. Anon. Boston: Warren Press, August 1944. 58 leaves, gray hardcover with gold printing and decoration, 27.3 x 20.3 cm, photos, ports., roster. SCM.

745 *The Memo: Navy Supply Corps Midshipmen Officers' School, Harvard Graduate School of Business Administration.* Cover: Memo. Bob Gray ed. N.p., 27 September 1944. 60 leaves, blue and white hardcover with gold printing and eagle, 27.4 x 20.4 cm, photos, ports., roster. SCM.

746 *An Account Current of the Class of October 1944, Navy Supply Corps School, Harvard University.* Cover: Account Current: October 1944, Navy Supply Corps, Harvard University. Earle W. Newton and Larry Chervenak, eds. N.p., October 1944. 64 leaves, blue hardcover with gold printing and decoration, 27.1 x 20.2 cm, photos, ports., roster. SCM.

747 *Account Current: Class Book of the Navy Supply Corps School, Harvard University, January 1945.* Cover: Account Current: January 1945, Navy Supply Corps School, Harvard University. Ens. Weldon Brewer, ed. N.p., January 1945. 50 leaves, blue hardcover with gold printing and decoration, 27.2 x 20.3 cm, photos, ports., roster. SCM.

748 *Account Current: Classbook of the Navy Supply Corps School, Harvard University, March 1945*. Cover: Account Current: Navy Supply Corps School, Harvard University, March 1945. Herbert L. Carpenter, Jr., ed. N.p., March 1945. 133 pp., blue hardcover with gold printing and decoration, 27.2 x 20.3 cm, photos, ports., roster. SCM.

749 *Account Current: Navy Supply Corps School, Harvard University, June 1945*. Cover: Account Current: June 1945, 1795–1945. Charles J. Parker, ed. N.p., June 1945. 123 pp., blue hardcover with gold printing and decoration, 27.2 x 20.3 cm, photos, ports., roster. SCM.

750 *Memo: Navy Supply Corps Midshipmen Officers' School, July 1945 Harvard Graduate School of Business Administration*. Cover: Memo. James R. Worsley, Jr., Graham B. Moody, Jr., and James Tillotson, eds. Boston: Warren Press, July 1945. 112 pp., blue hardcover with gold printing and decoration, 27.2 x 20.3 cm, photos, ports., roster. SCM.

751 *Account Current: Classbook of the Navy Supply Corps School, Harvard University, August 1945*. Cover: Account Current. Vincent H. Anderson, ed. N.p., August 1945. 120 pp., blue hardcover with gold printing and decoration, 27.2 x 20.3 cm, photos, ports., roster. SCM.

752 *Account Current: Class of December 1945, Navy Supply Corps School, Harvard University*. Cover: Account Current: Navy Supply Corps School, December 1945. Frank Axe, William Read, and H. Baird Tenney, eds. N.p., December 1945. 84 pp., blue and white hardcover with gold printing and decoration, 27.2 x 20.5 cm, photos, ports., roster. SCM.

753 *The Account Current: The Yearbook of the Class of February 1946, Navy Supply Corps School, Harvard University*. Cover: Account Current: Navy Supply Corps School, February 1946. Robert R. Eckert, ed. N.p., February 1946. 136 pp., blue hardcover with gold printing and decoration, 27.2 x 20.5 cm, photos, ports., roster. SCM.

754 *The Account Current of the Navy Supply Corps School, June 1946*. Cover: Account Current: June 1946. R. F. Delaney, ed. N.p., June 1946. 80 pp., light green hardcover with blue printing, 27.2 x 20.2 cm, photos, ports., roster. SCM.

Naval Supply Corps School, Wellesley College, Wellesley, Massachusetts

755 *The Memo: Classbook of Navy Supply Corps School, February 1944, Wellesley Unit—Wellesley College, Wellesley, Massachusetts.* Cover: The Memo: Navy Supply Corps School, Wellesley Unit, February 1944. Francis Xavier Ahearn, ed. N.p., February 1944. 32 pp., blue hardcover with gold printing, 27.1 x 20 cm, photos, ports., roster. SCM.

756 *Smooth Roll: The United States Navy Supply Corps School, Wellesley College, Wellesley, Massachusetts.* Cover: Smooth Roll: Navy Supply Corps School, Wellesley Unit, April 1944. Donnell Davis, ed. N.p., April 1944. 20 leaves, blue hardcover with gold printing, 27.1 x 20.2 cm, photos, ports., roster. SCM.

757 *Specimen No. 4: Navy Supply Corps School, Wellesley College, April to September Nineteen Forty-four.* Cover: Specimen No. 4: Navy Supply Corps School, Wellesley College. R. K. Arnold, ed. N.p., September 1944. 56 pp., light blue hardcover with gold printing, 27.3 x 20.2 cm, photos, ports., roster. SCM.

758 *The Welnav: The United States Navy Supply Corps School, Wellesley Unit, Wellesley, Massachusetts.* Cover: The Welnav: June 1944. Ferd A. Glojek, ed. N.p., June 1944. 21 leaves plus advertising section, blue hardcover with gold printing and decoration, 27.4 x 20 cm, photos, ports., map, roster. SCM.

Naval Supply Depot, Chimu Wan Tengan, Okinawa

759 *Okinawa Memories: Naval Supply Depot, Chimu Wan Tengan, Okinawa* (cover). Anon. N.p., [1946?]. 32 pp., 19 x 26.6 cm, photos, ports. NDL (photocopy).

Naval Supply Depot, New Orleans, Louisiana

760 *U.S. Naval Supply Depot, New Orleans, Louisiana, 1945* (cover). Anon. Baton Rouge: Army & Navy Publishing Co., 1946. 117 pp., embossed blue hardcover with gold printing and emblem, 30.8 x 23.3 cm, photos, ports., roster. NDL.

Naval Supply Depot, Norfolk, Virginia

761 *War History, Naval Supply Depot, Norfolk, Virginia.* Cover: War History of Naval Supply Depot, Norfolk. Anon. N.p., [1946?]. 185 pp., blue hardcover with gold printing and plant sketch, 25.6 x 32.9 cm, photos, ports. NDL.

Naval Supply Depot, Oakland, California

762 *Naval Supply Depot, Oakland, 1941–1945.* Cover: Power for the Pacific Punch: Naval Supply Depot, Oakland. Planning Division NSD, Oakland. N.p., October 1945. 43 leaves, printed on one side of sheet only, gray paper cover with red and black printing and cartoon decoration, spiral binding, 29.9 x 22.3 cm, photos. SCM.

763 *Wartime History of the Supply Corps: U.S. Naval Supply Depot, Oakland, California, as of 31 December 1944.* Anon. N.p., 1945. 352 pp., blue binding, 27.6 x 21.5 cm, typed manuscript with photographs tipped in. SCM. This is not a true cruise book but a history of Oakland Supply Depot operations during WW II.

Naval Supply Depot, San Pedro, California

764 *War History of the U.S. Naval Supply Depot, San Pedro, California.* Cover: War History of the United States Naval Supply Depot, San Pedro, California. Anon. U.S. Naval Supply Depot, publisher. N.p., [1946?]. 81 pp., blue hardcover with gold printing and emblem, 23.4 x 30.9 cm, photos, ports. NDL.

Other Commands and Facilities

Advanced Intelligence Center

765 *AIC Days.* Anon. N.p., [1945?]. 36 pp., photos. Q. M. Dabney Catalogue 361 [August 1990?]. No known copy location.

Argus 16 Tarawa

766 *This Was ~~Is~~ Pastel.* Lt. Robert E. Anderson, USNR, ed. N.p., [1947?]. 16 leaves, blue hardcover with dark blue printing, 27.4 x 20.7 cm, photos, map, roster. NDL.

Armed Guard School, Shelton, Virginia

767 *Armed Guard School, Shelton, Virginia, September 1943* (page 17). Cover: The Plane Shooter Armed Guard School, Shelton, Virginia. Anon. Baton Rouge: Army & Navy Publishing Co., [1943?]. 63 pp., embossed blue hardcover, 30.9 x 23.3 cm, photos, ports. NDL.

768 *Armed Guard School, Shelton, Virginia* (page 17). Cover: The Plane Shooter Armed Guard School, Shelton, Virginia. Anon. Baton Rouge: Army & Navy Publishing Co., [1945?]. 113 pp., embossed blue hardcover with gold printing and emblem, 30.9 x 23.3 cm, photos, ports., roster. NDL.

Barracks (WR), Balboa Park, San Francisco, California

769 *USN Barracks (WR), Balboa Park, San Francisco, Commissioned July 1945, Decommissioned September 1946.* Cover: USS Balboa Ship's Log. Sp(E)(RW)1c Jean M. Boulet, ed. San Francisco: Bertrands Lithography and Printing Co., [1946?]. 52 pp., white paper cover with black printing, 28.6 x 22 cm, photos, ports. TIL. This facility was a barracks for WAVES and nurses.

CUB 16 (mobile fleet base unit)

770 *CUB Sixteen, 1944–45.* Anon. Baton Rouge: Army & Navy Publishing Co., [1946?]. 72 pp., embossed blue hardcover with gold printing and emblem, 30.8 x 23.4 cm, photos, ports., roster. NDL. This facility was an advanced supply and support unit.

Fighter Director Unit (See entry 766.)

Fleet Service Schools, Norfolk, Virginia

771 *Fleet Service Schools, Norfolk, Virginia* (cover). Anon. Baton Rouge: Army & Navy Publishing Co., [1946?]. 88 pp., embossed blue hardcover with gold printing and silhouette of ship, 30.8 x 23.3 cm, photos, ports., roster. NDL.

Naval Barracks, Mare Island Navy Yard, California

772 *United States Naval Barracks Naval Ammunition Depot, Mare Island/Vallejo, California.* N.p., n.d. 40 pp., 26.5 x 19.5 cm, photos. NDL.

Naval Mine Depot, Yorktown, Virginia

773 *Naval Mine Depot, Yorktown, Virginia, 1945* (cover). Anon. Baton Rouge: Army & Navy Publishing Co., 1945. 137 pp., embossed blue hardcover with gold printing and decoration of a mine, 30.9 x 23.3 cm, photos, ports., roster. NDL.

Naval Operating Base, Argentia, Newfoundland

774 *Argentia Sentinel of the North Atlantic, Navy 103* (cover). Anon. N.p., [1945?]. 64 leaves, embossed blue hardcover with gold printing and embossed view of ship and plane off Newfoundland, 23.4 x 31.3 cm, photos, ports. NDL, SMPH, USNA.

Naval Operating Base, Guam

775 *Lion Six*. Capt. D. Harry Hammer, USNR. Annapolis: United States Naval Institute, 1947. 109 pp., dust jacket, blue hardcover with gold printing and silhouette of lion, 25.5 x 17.8 cm, photos, ports., map. Smith: 9269, Zeigler: 2596. NDL, private collection.

Naval Receiving Station, Norfolk, Virginia

776 *U.S. Naval Receiving Station, 7800 Hampton Blvd., Norfolk, VA, 1945* (cover). Anon. Baton Rouge: Army & Navy Publishing Co., 1945. 106 pp., embossed blue hardcover with gold printing and anchor decoration, 30.9 x 23.3 cm, photos, ports., roster of transient personnel. NDL (volume 8). Nineteen volumes of this book were issued, each with different rosters and photographs of transient personnel.

Naval Repair Base, New Orleans, Louisiana

777 *Naval Repair Base, New Orleans, Louisiana (P & T Command)*. Baton Rouge: Army & Navy Publishing Co., [1946?]. Army & Navy Publishing Co. List. No known copy location.

Naval Training and Distribution Center, San Francisco

778 *The Naval History of Treasure Island*. Cover: The Naval History of Treasure Island. Lt. Comdr. E. A. McDevitt, ed. Treasure Island, Calif., 1946. 282 pp., brown and gray hardcover with multiple small views, 25.6 x 17.3 cm, photos, ports. Private collection.

Naval Training and Distribution Center, Shoemaker, California

779 *U.S. Navy* (cover). Anon. Baton Rouge: Army & Navy Publishing Co., n.d. 91 pp., embossed blue hardcover with gold printing and anchor, 30.9 x 23.5 cm, photos, ports., roster of transient personnel with photographs. NDL (volumes 7, 9, 12, 16, 17, 18, 19, 23, 26, 28, and 29). Private collection (volume 8). Thirty volumes of this book were published, each with different rosters of transient personnel.

Naval Training School (Indoctrination), Camp Macdonough, Plattsburg, New York

780 *Naval Training School (Indoctrination), Camp Macdonough, Plattsburg, NY*. Cover: The Q–12 Log: Naval Training School (Indoctrination), Camp Macdonough, Plattsburg, N.Y. Anon. [Baton Rouge: Army & Navy Publishing Co., 1945?]. 106 pp., embossed blue hardcover with gold printing and decoration, 30.9 x 23.3 cm, photos, ports., roster. NDL. The NDL has three different editions of this book. All are identical except for different rosters and minor changes.

Naval Training Station, Newport, Rhode Island

781 *Golden Boot: The Class Book of the Officers Indoctrination School, Naval Training Station, Newport, Rhode Island*. Cover: Golden Boot. Ens. James H. Shoemaker, USNR, et al., eds. N.p., November 1942. 191 pp., blue hardcover with gold printing and decoration, 27.5 x 20.8 cm, photos, ports., roster. NDL.

Naval Training Station, Sampson, New York

782 *The Making of a Sailor*. Cover: U.S. Naval Training Station, Sampson, N.Y. Richard Bennett Talcott, author and publisher. N.p., 1944. 24 leaves, blue and white paper-cover with photograph of sailors carrying base and U.S. flags, spiral binding, 26.7 x 20.3 cm, photos, ports. Private collection.

Navy Fleet Post Office, New York, New York

783 *United States Navy Fleet Post Office, New York, N.Y.* (cover). Anon. New York: Pictorial Lithographers, March 1946. 39 pp., blue softcover with red printing and emblem, 20.7 x 25.7 cm, photos, ports. Private collection.

Navy Fleet Post Office, San Francisco, California

784 *Souvenir Booklet Fleet Post Office San Francisco California*. Martha Piper Thomas, ed. San Francisco: [1946?]. 36 pp., Controvich 1992. No known copy location.

Navy Overseas Freight Terminal, San Francisco, California

785 *U.S. Navy Overseas Freight Terminal, San Francisco, California, 1941–1945*. Cover: Navy Overseas Freight Terminal, San Francisco. John D. McDonald, ed. Berkeley: Lederer Street & Zeus, [1946?]. 80 pp., blue hardcover with gold printing and decoration, photos, ports., roster. Private collection.

Navy Section Base, Tompkinsville, Staten Island, New York

786 *U.S. Navy Section Base, Tompkinsville, Staten Island, New York, April 1, 1943* (cover). Anon. N.p., April 1, 1943. 27 pp., amber color softcover with black printing and emblem decoration. No known copy location.

Transportation Pool 12 ND, Treasure Island, California

787 *History of Transportation Pool 12 ND, U.S. Naval Training and Distribution Center, Treasure Island, California.* Cover: Transportation Pool 12 ND, U.S. Naval Training and Distribution Center, Treasure Island, California. Violet A. Mattes. San Francisco: 1946. 42 pp., blue hardcover with gold printing, 25.8 x 20.8 cm, photos, ports., roster. SMPH.

WAVES (Women Accepted for Volunteer Emergency Service)

788 *WAVES United States Navy* (cover). Anon. Baton Rouge: Army & Navy Publishing Co., [1946?]. 92 pp., embossed blue hardcover with gold printing and anchor in white, 30.9 x 23.3 cm, photos, ports., roster with photographs. NDL. There are several editions of this book. They differ only in the rosters. Those in NDL include:

1) WAVES Overseas Unit, Company J, Shoemaker, California

2) Woman's Reserve Overseas Unit, U.S. Naval Training and Distribution Center, Shoemaker, California

3) WAVES Overseas Unit, Company C, USN TADCEN, Shoemaker, California

4) WAVE Detachment Overseas Unit, Company E, Shoemaker, California, 1945

5) WAVE Detachment Overseas Unit, Company F, Shoemaker, California, 1945

World War II's Navy Demolition Research Unit

789 *World War II's Navy Demolition Research Unit, Ft. Pierce, Florida* (cover). Lt. (jg) Charles J. Henstock, ed. N.p., [1946?]. 28 leaves, printed on one side of page only, tan paper cover with black printing and eagle, 25.8 x 20.2 cm, photos, ports., roster. Dornbusch 1950: 1069. NYPL.

Index of Naval Commands

☆ U.S. GOVERNMENT PRINTING OFFICE: 1993 331–311